# Grief Expressed

## *When a Mate Dies*

### MARTA FELBER

**LifeWords**

**Library of Congress Catalog Card Number: 2007906787**
ISBN 978-0-9799214-0-7

First Printing: 1997 by LifeWords
Second Printing: 2002 by Fairview Press
Third Printing: 2008 by LifeWords
Printed in the United States of America

**LifeWords**
419 Salem Vista Ct.
Winston-Salem, NC 27101
www.LifeWords.com

The poem *Home* appearing on page iv is used with the permission of the author, Kay Winters.

Design and production:     John Coghlan
Cover photography:         Tim Ernst, Background; Don House, Foreground
Text photography:          Karl Sandrock, pages 30, 31, 80, and 81; Don House, page viii
Screened images:           Corel

# *Dedication*

TO JOE, my husband and best friend, whose death gave birth to this book—
you taught me the meaning of true love and made our years together
joy-filled. A part of you remains with me. . . . I love you.

TO MARGE, my "counselor" friend—you have always listened, but given no
advice. Your faith in me has given me the courage to go on many times. Your
positive approach to life is contagious. . . . I thank you.

TO KAY, my friend, whose love of life has inspired me to find my own joy in
living—our joint adventures in faraway places provided memories to get
through rough times. I applaud your writing successes. . . . I treasure you.

# *Appreciation*

To the WIDOWED PERSONS in eight states in the U.S. who field-tested the
earliest set of exercises for this book—the investment of yourself and your
positive feedback encouraged me to go forward with the project.

# HOME

Home was such a refuge
When he was there.
You felt the welcome
Shared the warmth
And knew the meaning.

Now,
Home seems like a place
You have to go
Don't want to stay.
Are glad to leave.

In time, you'll redefine
Rearrange
Reassess and find
That home is where you are
And choose to be.

Your refuge.

Kay Winters

# Step by Step

# About the Author

Marta Felber has drawn from her counseling background for self-healing since the death of her husband. She has held counseling positions in Pennsylvania, Arkansas, Egypt, and Indonesia and worked as a consultant at international schools in Nepal, India, and Bangladesh. During her ten years in Indonesia, Marta served as director and head counselor at a center for expatriates in Jakarta.

Marta has three sons and four grandchildren. She lives in northwest Arkansas, where she takes daily walks in the gentle Ozark Mountains. She continues writing for publication. *Finding Your Way after Your Spouse Dies* is her second book for those who are on their personal journey through grief.

Dear Fellow Traveler,

We who have lost mates are traveling the road of grief, moving toward acceptance of that reality. We are affirming our identities, apart from those of our loved ones. We are taking control of our lives.

*Grief Expressed: When a Mate Dies* contains the written work I completed on my journey. You are invited to journey with me, "touch my grief," and then do what is best for you.

These exercises were begun in a hospital room where my husband lay dying from a rare and incurable brain disease. Two spiral notebooks were by my side at all times. I wrote my feelings and how I might deal with the problems ahead. After his death I continued this process. The work I share with you is what I experienced and planned.

There is no one right way to work through grief. Each person must find his or her own way. WRITING my feelings and solutions helped me. It brought into focus the multitude of issues that confronted me. Later I could return to what I had written for reinforcement, for direction, and to make additions.

You are free to use what I have written as a SPRINGBOARD for your thoughts and feelings. Also, you may COPY anything from what I have written if it fits how you feel or what you choose to do. The moment you put it on your page, IT IS YOURS.

Resist the temptation to skip over a given exercise. Deal with those from earlier stages and feel good about how you handled them. You may discover unfinished work you need to complete. Resisting an exercise in your present stage may mean you need to face it. Become familiar with upcoming exercises in the book so you can refer to them when you are ready.

Your situation is not the same as mine. DON'T GET SIDETRACKED by how I dealt with an issue. Make the exercises on your page FIT YOU. Change the title and headings to match what you need to do. Make up exercises of your own. Beginning on page 111, you'll find reading and resources for additional help. Above all, do the SUMMARY STATEMENTS at the end of every exercise. They pull together and make sense of what you have done, giving you direction and instant replay as you read them again and again.

Perhaps you would like to share *Grief Expressed* with another person or a group. Additional copies of this book can be ordered through Fairview Press (1-800-544-8207).

YOU ARE SPECIAL AND DESERVE TO BE FREE.

*Marta*

Marta Felber

# NOBODY'S HOME
## *And I Don't Want to Go There*

The few things I needed were already in the supermarket cart. I looked at my watch. I had been wandering aimlessly up and down the aisles for thirty minutes, not choosing any groceries, not remembering anything I'd seen. And then I realized I didn't want to go home. Why should I? Joe wasn't there.

## Ways to Make the House Seem Less Empty

Use a radio alarm to hear a voice when I wake up.

Turn on the radio before I leave.

Plan something pleasant to do as soon as I get home. Read a book, brew herbal tea, call a friend, take a bubble bath.

Leave a light on to welcome me home.

Consider getting a pet: dog, cat, bird, or maybe fish.

Invite someone to my house each week for coffee, a meal, or a project.

Buy some houseplants and talk to each one. (It's supposed to make them flourish and grow.)

Interact with someone every day, on the phone or in person.

Change the area where he always sat to make it look different.

Using the *TV Guide*, make a viewing schedule for the week.

Plan dates with friends and things to do to get out of the house. Try to balance these outings so I don't have too many days home alone.

**Summary Statement:** To acknowledge that I hate to go home helps me face the emptiness and do something about it. I can start today by doing some of the things I have listed above. I will check this list from time to time and add other ideas.

# NOBODY'S HOME

*And I Don't Want to Go There*

How I feel about going home and the emptiness there:

Ways to Make the House Seem Less Empty

Summary Statement:

# FEELING SAFE
## *There Are Things I Can Do*

I never worried about someone breaking in or my personal safety while Joe was alive. That changed overnight. Suddenly I felt fearful and vulnerable. One of the first things I did after his death was install a blind on the bedroom window. I lower it at dusk. Even taking such a small step to protect myself makes me feel more secure.

## I Make It Safe

Install an additional security light on the house to shine over a larger area.

Keep doors locked both day and night.

Get a reliable flashlight and put in the drawer by bed. Check the batteries.

Consider an alarm system. Talk with people who have one. Research recommended systems in *Consumer Reports* at the library.

Install a peephole in front door.

Put my house number at the entrance to my driveway.

Purchase a cellular phone for the bedroom and car.

List the phone numbers of persons to call in an emergency. Have written directions to my house posted by my phone.

Check the availability and content of self-defense classes.

Purchase a key chain with mace or pepper spray.

Put a can of flat-tire fixer and flares in the trunk of my car.

Lock my car doors. Park in a lighted area; pay attention to people nearby when coming or going. Consider a remote-control car security light.

Continue my automobile club insurance.

**Summary Statement:** No one is ever totally safe, but as I choose to take additional safety precautions, I expect to gradually feel more secure. It is a relief to realize how many things I can do to help ensure my safety. Many can be done immediately.

# FEELING SAFE

*There Are Things I Can Do*

How safe do I feel?


Additional Safety Measures for Me


Summary Statement:

# WALKING "DOWN" TIMES AWAY
## *I Need to Exercise*

What has happened to my good health habits? An inner voice keeps nagging, "You've got to start reclaiming your body." I am aware of my loss of appetite, sleeplessness, fatigue, depression, and low energy level. I have decided to try WALKING THESE THINGS AWAY.

## How Do I Get Started

FIND A WALKING FRIEND. My motivation is at zero. A partner would help. If I promise I will meet a friend at a certain time, I will do it.

START SLOWLY. I must listen to my body when it tells me I've had enough. In the beginning, it may be better to take two short walks in a day than one long one. I can gradually increase my pace and distance.

WALK REGULARLY. It is important for me to establish the habit, even if it's only a short walk. I will start with three days a week and then add more.

WALK EARLY. It would be a good way to get myself started in the morning. I find this very difficult right now. An exercise program will also increase my energy level for the rest of the day.

MAKE A RAINY DAY PLAN. Ride a stationary bike and read. Use an exercise tape. Mall walk, alone or with a friend.

SPICE IT UP. Use a Walkman and play music that has a rhythm that matches my mood. Plan something fun to do after the walk with my partner. Vary the walking route.

**Summary Statement:** I know I would feel better if I got regular exercise. It would add structure to my life. I would feel more like eating and also sleep better. It would be great to have more energy. Jan loves to walk; I'll call her and see if she can go walking tomorrow!

# WALKING "DOWN" TIMES AWAY

*I Need to Exercise*

What an exercise program could do for me:

My Exercise Choice and Plan for Getting Started

**Summary Statement:**

# I HAVE; I OWE

## *Where Am I Financially?*

A bill arrives, and then another, sometimes several in one day! I start to panic. Is there enough money? Will I be able to pay my bills? How many more can I expect? What do I do if the money runs short? I must take time for a quick calculation of my income and what I owe. The reality may not be as bad as I fear. I also need a simple, immediate plan of action.

**I Have**                                                              **I Owe**

## Plan of Action

Place all bills, financial statements, requests for money, and anything else related to finances into a box or drawer that is used only for that purpose. Do this every day as soon as I get the mail.

Twice a month, go through every item. (Pull out estate-settling items. I choose to get professional help with these.) Pay bills first, in order of importance. Make arrangements for any bills I cannot pay. Deal with the rest, all in one day if possible.

Balance my checkbook against my bank statement on the fifteenth of every month.

Try not to worry about finances the rest of the month. If those nagging thoughts begin, I can say to myself, "I have a designated time for dealing with that."

**Summary Statement:** The above quick tabulation and plan of action will get me by for now. Most major financial decisions can wait until I can think more clearly and have the information I need. In my present condition I could make costly mistakes. I need to move slowly and deliberately and be in control. I won't let anyone pressure me into anything. When I am ready I will get help from informed persons who do not have vested interests. I am in charge of getting and using that help. Later, I will take a course on managing finances.

(See books on handling finances under Recommended Reading and Resources at the back of this book.)

# I HAVE; I OWE

*Where Am I Financially?*

I Have                                                          I Owe

Plan of Action

**Summary Statement:**

# MY WORLD TURNED UPSIDE DOWN

## *On That Terrible Day*

It had been gloomy and rainy for days, but the sun came out that morning. How dare the sun shine when he lay there dying and would never enjoy sunshine again!

## Tell It Again, One More Time

It was a Saturday, but days of the week had lost their significance. What mattered was that he was still breathing, long past the time the doctors had given him to live. For five long weeks I had kept my vigil, day and night in that hospital room. I knew that it would be our last "home." It was here that I had made the hardest decision of my life, to sign for the removal of the life support system. It seemed as if I was taking his very life away. I had held out on this decision for more than a week, against the counsel of his doctors and the reality of all the tests. Finally, I had agreed to let him go, and still he lived.

I did not know that it was his last day when I washed his face and combed his hair, as I had done every morning. I had long before learned not to expect him to know I was there or to make any response.

I had struggled the night before, back and forth, back and forth, wanting him to die for his sake, and wanting him to live because I didn't think I could live without him. Finally, after many prayers I was able to say, "God will take him in His and Joe's own time. I can neither hurry it nor keep it from happening. I let it be." And, for the first time since his illness began, I was at peace.

It was as if he waited until I had reached that place of peace. He breathed evenly while I ate a few bites of the breakfast that the staff had brought to the room for me. Then I heard the irregular breathing pattern. The doctor had told me that this would be the only signal that death was near. I hurried to the bed and held him in my arms while he took those last breaths. I told him of my love, confident his hovering spirit would hear. . . . When my final good-byes seemed complete, I lowered him to the bed and pressed the nurses' call button.

Joe's life was over, and my life without him began.

**Summary Statement:** As awful as that day was, my one wish was granted, to hold him as he died. I look back on that day and say, "Joe's was a calm passing, and Marta, you did for him all you could."

# MY WORLD TURNED UPSIDE DOWN
## *On That Terrible Day*

## Tell It Again, One More Time

**Summary Statement:**

# IT DIDN'T HELP WHEN THEY SAID

## *Those Words of "Comfort"*

During the early days of grieving, it seemed as if nobody could say anything helpful. It was not their fault. I was in such pain that I was quick to misunderstand words that were kindly meant. It is difficult to know what will be comforting when a person is grieving. Thinking back to those early days, I remember their comments and my inner responses.

| When They Said | I Thought/Felt |
|---|---|
| "You're looking great!" | That can't be true. I feel dreadful. If I do look great, what's wrong? |
| "I'm so proud of you." | I must come through and act like I feel fine. That's what they expect. |
| "How are you today?" | Terrible. But I don't think you want to hear that. |
| "You must be really busy. I called you several times and you weren't home." | Do they think I am out socializing, getting over his death too soon? |
| "Let me know if there's anything I can do." | Please think of something to offer because I can't. I'm hurting too much to know what I want or need. |
| "You're doing just fine." | Am I being complimented for having "gotten over it?" Please let me grieve. |
| "Remember, it could be worse. He could have lingered longer." | What does it matter when he went? He's gone. Can't you understand? |
| "Joe is waiting for you over there. Some day you will be with him." | Maybe so; who knows really? I want him so much now. I don't want to die to be with him. |
| "I know just how you feel." | No, you don't. No one knows exactly how awful I feel and how much I miss him. |

**Summary Statement:** Maybe I need to listen to what people mean, instead of what they say. Just accept that they are reaching out in the only way they know, to show they care.

# IT DIDN'T HELP WHEN THEY SAID

## *Those Words of "Comfort"*

When They Said                                        I Thought/Felt

**Summary Statement:**

# HOW TO MAKE IT THROUGH THE NIGHT

### *It Seems Endless*

I can pretend during the daytime that Joe is away, working outside, or in his workshop. Alone for the evening meal and crawling into an empty bed confirm the worst! The loneliness for him descends like a shroud and there is no escape. What do I do to get to sleep easier? And what about those long hours in the middle of the night when I wake and can't get back to sleep?

## Ideas for Getting to Sleep and Surviving the Long Nights

STICK TO A REGULAR SCHEDULE. Have dinner with the TV news commentator. Have a set time to go to bed, a radio alarm to wake me at the same time every morning. Get up, regardless of how little sleep I have had. Maybe take an early afternoon nap, not longer than thirty minutes; set the timer.

GET REGULAR EXERCISE EVERY DAY, but not within three hours of going to bed. Exercise relieves stress and may help me relax and fall asleep.

AVOID CAFFEINE AND ALCOHOL. In addition to regular coffee, there are measurable amounts of caffeine in chocolate, some soft drinks, and nonherbal tea. It is a stimulant that can interfere with sleep. Alcohol disturbs sleep patterns.

EAT LIGHT AT THE EVENING MEAL. Have a carbohydrate snack about an hour before bedtime. Also try a glass of milk.

AVOID SLEEPING PILLS. It is too easy to become dependent and too difficult to get off them.

GET SUNLIGHT IN THE AFTERNOON. It helps my body's natural clock let me sleep at night.

CREATE A SLEEP-PRODUCING ATMOSPHERE: Low lighting, soothing music, a tepid bath, deep breathing, visualization of a beautiful setting, relaxation of body muscles, or inspirational reading. Develop a nightly ritual of the things that work for me.

BESIDE MY BED, for those long wakeful hours, put dull reading material, a journal to record my feelings, note cards, a note pad for "to do" lists, a manicure set, and a radio for late night talk shows and music.

IF ALL ELSE FAILS, go to the kitchen and make hot chocolate, adding marshmallows. Sip slowly, listen to the night sounds, look for the moon, the stars. Remember that nighttime is a good time for crying, and crying is healing.

**Summary Statement:** I only need to get through one night at a time. I can do this. When I wake during the night, I will determine if I need to cry, get busy, prepare food, or just feel God's presence and a place of peace. Morning will come.

# HOW TO MAKE IT THROUGH THE NIGHT

## *It Seems Endless*

### Ideas for Getting to Sleep and Surviving the Long Nights

**Summary Statement:**

# EVERYWHERE I LOOK

## *There Are Reminders*

Why do I feel sad when I use the remote control? Maybe I know why. Joe always "ran" the TV while I watched and did mindless tasks. The remote is a symbol of all the jobs that were his that I had to take over, and that fact confirms his death.

## Symbols and What They Mean

JOE'S CLIPBOARD. Reminds me of his profession, abilities, and special talents. How unfair it is that all were taken away. I grieve for this loss.

HIS COFFEE MUG. Embodies all our snacks and meals, his food preferences, and our eating out. Eating time is unbearably lonely now.

OLD SPICE MUSK DEODORANT. When he held me I was always aware of his "smell." How I miss all those hugs and close body times.

STATUE OF OLD MAN. He picked this out on one of our trips. It reminds me of our travels. Those times were so much fun! I mourn the loss of my traveling buddy and all the trips we had planned.

HIS TOOTHBRUSHES. How conscientious he was about taking care of his teeth. I admired that. Good health was important to him. So why did he get sick and die?

PLAID HAT. It hangs in the entryway and reminds me of all the things he did and enjoyed outdoors. I can see him on the tractor, gathering wood, and taking a walk. His hat gives me a warm feeling.

TOOLBOX. Next to me, he loved his tools best! He did the finishing work in our home. It still hurts to look around and see his handiwork, but some day it will be a comfort.

**Summary Statement:** From now on I will let the feelings come that surround these symbols. Only then am I free to hold these feelings or to let them go.

# EVERYWHERE I LOOK
## *There Are Reminders*

When I See (Objects)                                    I Think/Feel

**Summary Statement:**

# WHERE ARE THE FRIENDS

## *Who Were So Close?*

Our closest friends were out of the country when Joe died. The husband called as soon as they heard the news. After their initial expressions of caring, there was a dropping off of contact to almost nothing. I was so disappointed and hurt. This happened with some other friends, too. I am trying to understand.

## My Friends Have Disappeared Because:

They care about me and want to make it all right again. But they can't "fix it," and this presents a hopeless situation.

Our lifestyles are no longer the same. I am no longer part of a couple. I'm dealing with probate, interpreting insurance forms, and wrestling with finances. They cannot relate to where I am.

Some people are not comfortable handling their own feelings, much less my feelings.

Joe's death is a threat to their own mortality. If he died, so will they. This is too difficult to handle.

They want me to be finished with my grieving and I'm not. Their time limit for me has expired.

My very presence is a reminder of Joe's death. It is more comfortable if I am not where they can see me right now.

They have not lost a mate, so they cannot possibly appreciate the depth of my grief. Earlier, I would not have understood either.

In my condition, I don't fit into light social gatherings. I can't seem to pull myself "up," and they resent being pulled "down."

They think that finding another companion for me is the perfect solution. They try to set this up, and I'm not ready.

**Summary Statement:** I understand why these friendships are diminishing. It is probably related more to the situation and where they are, than to me. A few friends have remained. They are treasured beyond measure. I am also making new friends who understand my grief. These select friends form a support circle around me. Later, I may reconnect with some of my former friends.

# WHERE ARE THE FRIENDS
*Who Were So Close?*

## Friends Who Have "Gone Away"

## Why They Have Gone

## New Friends and What They Mean to Me

## Former Friends with Whom I Will Reconnect

**Summary Statement:**

# I WANT TO BE PREPARED

## *For Those Unwanted Advances*

No way was I prepared for those subtle, and not so subtle, advances from men in the early months after Joe's death. There weren't many, but they were unsettling. I want to know what to do if they happen again.

| Advances | Ways to Handle |
| --- | --- |
| A man sitting next to me at the table inched closer and kept rubbing his leg against mine. | Change seats, if possible. Go to the ladies' room. |
| Men let their hands linger at my waist or around my shoulders much longer than appropriate. | Remove the hand. If it is happens again, say, "Please don't do that." |
| Men make suggestive off-color remarks or jokes. They would never have done this if Joe had been there. | Ignore it the first time. If it happens again, say, "I don't appreciate hearing that." Change the subject. |

## Feelings That Surfaced

| | |
| --- | --- |
| Surprise | I did not expect this to happen so soon! |
| Invaded | I don't want him in my space! |
| Cheap | What does he think I am? |
| Angry | How dare he! |
| Defensive | Leave me alone! |
| Guilty | Did I send him a message that I wanted this? |
| Frustration | I don't want to deal with this. |
| Defenseless | With no partner, am I free game? |
| Lonely | It's so hard to go out without Joe. |

**Summary Statement:** I need to take control of these situations. Being mentally and emotionally prepared will help me do this. It is also important to be in touch with my feelings.

# I WANT TO BE PREPARED
## *For Those Unwanted Advances*

Advances                                        Ways to Handle

### Feelings That Surfaced

**Summary Statement:**

# JUST SAY NO

## *And Make Time for Grieving*

It's hard for me to say no. With the best of intentions, many people want to keep me busy. It's their "cure" for my missing Joe. I, too, thought I must get involved, and my calendar is filled. What I really need is more time to be alone and let myself grieve.

## Just Say No To:

POTLUCK SUPPERS. I don't feel like preparing food or making small talk. I would rather stay home with a good book.

SINGLES GROUPS. The members are younger. I don't feel like joining in the discussions, and the social events don't "fit" me now.

BRIDGE CLUB. It is too complicated. I don't need the pressure of competition.

AN EXTENDED TRIP WITH A GROUP. Instead, I'll start with a shorter one.

A DOG. It would be an added responsibility, and I don't want to be tied down now.

A JAZZ CONCERT. It is not my favorite kind of music. Why should I go just to have something to do?

CHURCH RESPONSIBILITY. Requires preparation every Sunday. I need to do something that is not so demanding, for now.

COMPUTER CLASS. I have wanted to do this for years, and I have the time, but it requires more concentration than I have now.

INVITING THE FAMILY FOR A HOLIDAY. It will bring back too many memories to handle. Maybe next year.

HOSPICE VOLUNTEERING. I must deal with my own grief first.

**Summary Statement:** I can do any of these later. My first priority is to deal with my grief. I can say no to any activity that is not in line with my goal, without feeling guilty. I will know when it feels right to go ahead.

# JUST SAY NO

*And Make Time for Grieving*

**Assessment of my activity level:**

**I Need to Say No To:**

**Summary Statement:**

# MY JOURNAL IS MY FRIEND
## *Always Near to "Hear" My Grief*

The pain is unbearable! I put down the feelings that engulf me. They come tumbling out, faster than I can write. Some words are blotted out where tears have fallen. I write the date and time of day before each entry, giving reality to what is happening. Sometimes I write a lot, other times only a sentence or two. Always I feel some measure of release.

**To You, the Reader:** You can begin a journal, writing your feelings on the next page. Note the date and time. Purchase a spiral notebook and continue writing through your grief and beyond.

## Why I Write in a Journal

My journal offers a ready release. It is always with me, going in my purse when I leave the house. My friends are not that available.

Having to write slows me down to a pace I can handle. It gets me off the treadmill of going nowhere.

My feelings get all jumbled. Writing helps me to separate them and to make sense of what is happening in my life.

Putting my problems on paper organizes them, and I can begin to write possible solutions. I can refer back and check my progress.

When I need to release pent-up feelings, I can read what I wrote in the early days. That will trigger the tears that need to flow.

Questions without answers can be written down and left on the paper. It stops them from going 'round and 'round in my head.

As my grief is released, I begin to note some breaks in the clouds. That feels so good.

A running chronicle gives me a "then" and "now" to measure my growth.

My journal is proof of my survival.

**Summary Statement:** This journal method of expressing my grief has helped me more than anything else. I will continue to share with my journal, a friend who is always near.

# MY JOURNAL IS MY FRIEND

*Always Near to "Hear" My Grief*

Date _____ Time of day_____

**Summary Statement:**

# HELP! I'M BEING BOMBARDED!

## *Disasters Hit All at Once*

The gas serviceman man found a leak and said, "You'll have to dig up the line from the tank to the house." My lawyer called and asked for two more documents, and I could not find either one. The painter was coming to stain the deck the next day and the loose boards had not been repaired. When I discovered ceiling tile coming down in the kitchen, indicating a leak above, I heard myself screaming, "I can't take it! It's too much! I give up!" I sobbed and sobbed.

## When Disasters Strike, I Can:

Cry until I feel the tension go.

Find a physical outlet: pound a pillow, slam the bathtub with a towel, or go for a brisk walk.

Call a good friend and unload.

Back up and handle (or choose not to handle) each problem in turn. Make a list of what needs to be done. This puts me back in control.

For each problem, contact a specialist for advice or assistance.

Get away, even if it is only for a few hours.

Keep on top of each disaster as soon as it happens.

Compare my problems with world disasters to keep my perspective.

**Summary Statement:** I can stockpile strength during the periods of calm. I will also use those times to work on my "to do" list. Bad times will come again, and when they do, I will share or release my frustrations and get specific help as soon as possible. These feelings of powerlessness will not last forever.

# HELP! I'M BEING BOMBARDED!

*Disasters Hit All at Once*

Disasters that have happened to me:

When Disasters Strike, I Can:

Summary Statement:

# SAME TIME AS LAST YEAR

## *But Entirely Different*

I don't want my birthday this year! Joe always did such thoughtful things. But he died two weeks ago. How do I face my birthday and all those other special days without him?

MY BIRTHDAY. I planned the day—breakfast out, browsing time in the library, a haircut and new style, birthday lunch at the nicest restaurant in town (with my book), and the purchase of a birthday gift (a padded cover for my exercise bike). The telephone was ringing when I got home. Friends near and far called with best wishes. In between calls I read the cards and letters I had saved. Missing Joe hit hard at bedtime, and it felt good to cry. I survived.

HIS BIRTHDAY. Anticipating that his birthday would be harder than mine, I had chosen this time for my friend to come from out of state. We went to Joe's favorite Mexican restaurant, where we toasted him with margaritas. I kept thinking, "The only way out is through." In between the tears I talked constantly about Joe, and my friend listened. I ordered his old standby meal. It seemed as if he should be sitting there in the booth with us. It hurt, but I'm glad we went.

OUR ANNIVERSARY. For months I dreaded the day. Should I pretend that it was any other day or plow right through the grief I felt? I chose to make it special and remember. My son agreed to go with me to the lovely restaurant where Joe and I had celebrated our anniversary many times. As the waitress got closer to the drapery-drawn private booth, I wanted to shout, "No, that booth is Joe's and mine!" I couldn't believe that we could sit through that long meal (in the booth that Joe and I always asked for), swap stories about Joe that the other had not heard, and not feel sad. Sometimes we laughed. Before going to bed that night, I read the cards that Joe had saved. They confirmed that I had told him over and over how much he meant to me. The day I had dreaded so much had turned out to be both beautiful and special.

THANKSGIVING. I took care of this holiday by working at the Salvation Army serving dinner to needy persons. Joe and I had talked about doing this but we never did. I worked this year for both of us.

CHRISTMAS. I knew I couldn't stay in our home for Christmas that first year without Joe. After my "have to" list was done, I ran away to Hot Springs, Arkansas, and stayed for three days in a hotel. I indulged myself in the famous thermal baths and got a massage. A Christmas Eve service on TV and telephone time with my family on Christmas Day was all of the holiday that I could handle. The rest of the time I read, cried, and ate chocolates. I allowed Christmas to flow around me that year. It was the best that I could do.

**Summary Statement:** For each special day I need to determine what I can and cannot handle. Then I plan, plan, plan. Dreading the days does not help and may be unwarranted. Each special day that I survive helps me to face the next one. I will start new rituals and traditions.

# SAME TIME AS LAST YEAR
## *But Entirely Different*

How I handled or will handle:

### Birthdays

### Our Anniversary

### Thanksgiving

### Other Holidays

### Special Days

**Summary Statement:**

# THE WORRIES GO 'ROUND AND 'ROUND

## *I Make Them Stop*

The box I was carrying down the stairs required two hands. I tripped and almost fell. I found myself trembling! What if I had fallen and really hurt myself? I could have laid there for days before someone found me. Worries about health, safety, and other matters go 'round in my head. I'll write them on the Worry Wheel and put them away. In a few months, I'll see what happened to my worries. Today's date **February 2**

Rim of Truth date

**August 4**

**Summary Statement:** Most of my worries have not come true. So why worry? Worries that I held on to became more entrenched. From now on, when a worry hits I will ask, "What can I do about this?" Then I will DO SOMETHING or LET IT GO!

30

# THE WORRIES GO 'ROUND AND 'ROUND

## *I Make Them Stop*

Write a worry that you have in each of the spokes of the wheel below. Choose ones which seem to go 'round and 'round in your head. Remember little ones as well as big ones. Try to put one in every spoke. Do not write in the outside rim of the wheel. Later write in the Rim of Truth what happened to each worry. Worry Wheel date _____

Rim of Truth date

_____

**Summary Statement:**

# FINDING STRENGTH TO GO ON

## *When My Feet Are Slipping*

Sometimes grief washes over me like waves, and I scramble for something solid. What can I count on?

## I Believe:

There is a God who cares about me and is with me all the time.

The sun will rise and set.
Spring will follow winter.
New life will emerge from buried bulbs.

My closest friends love and accept me as I am.

I am a worthwhile person.
I am intelligent, capable, with inner strength.

Tomorrow is a new day.

## My Beliefs Can Be Posted On:

The mirror of my dressing table.

A stand-up card on the table where I eat.

A card to use as a bookmark.

The frame of the computer screen.

The door of the microwave.

**Summary Statement:** As I stand on these beliefs, I can withstand the storms that will come.

# FINDING STRENGTH TO GO ON

### *When My Feet Are Slipping*

## I Believe:

## My Beliefs Can Be Posted On:

**Summary Statement:**

# BUILDING A SUPPORT SYSTEM

## *People I Can Depend On*

I need people in my life, for companionship, advice, and getting things done.

## I Have Someone For:

Repairs around the house:  Karl (son), Jim (handyman).

Home upkeep decisions:  Don (neighbor).

Car maintenance:  Jim (keeps twenty-seven-year-old "Francis" running smoothly).

Family problem sharing:  Marge, Kay (long-term friends).

Companion for plays, lectures, concerts:  Edith (new widow friend).

Travel companion:  Rozetta (who has been many places).

Elderhostel participant:  Betty (we attended our first one together).

Exercise coordinator:  Pat (water aerobics in her pool).

Financial help:  Jim (broker), Walter (CPA).

Legal assistance:  Jim (lawyer).

Landscaping:  LeAnn (does "natural" landscaping that I like).

Hair care:  Robert (created my new hair style).

Eating-out friend:  Jan (enjoys eating leisurely).

Shopping comrade:  Neva (appreciates finding great bargains too).

Weight control partner:  Peggy (monthly weigh-ins and inspiration).

Daily contact with the outside world:  Willa (postmistress).

Good book recommendations:  Juanita (librarian).

President of my fan club:  Marlene (thinks I'm wonderful and tells me).

Loving letter writer:  Hilde (from the other side of the world).

Emergency contact:  Karl (son: name, address, phone is in my wallet).

Medical consultant:  Dr. Cude (family doctor for many years).

Life-line to Joe:  Troy and Suzy (Joe's nephew and his wife).

**Summary Statement:** I have so many people on whom I can depend! I will add to this list as needs arise. For now it is okay to get all the help I can.

# BUILDING A SUPPORT SYSTEM
*People I Can Depend On*


**I Have Someone For:**


**Summary Statement:**

# I TALK TO MYSELF

## *Make It Nurturing*

It was cold in the mall parking lot, and the wind made it seem even colder. I half stumbled up and down the rows of parked cars searching for mine. As I walked I talked to myself. "Stupid! You can't remember anything! What's the matter with you? All you had to do was fix a landmark. You'll never find it if you start crying!" Later, as I sat in the car, I continued to hear the negative words.

## Negative Self-Talk

On a separate sheet of paper, I will keep a running list of self-criticisms and put-downs as I become aware of them.

## Nurturing Conversations with Myself

There is much on your mind. . . . It's easy to forget. . . . Perhaps next time you'll look for a landmark. . . . It's okay. . . . Give yourself time. . . . Your friends still love you, regardless of what you do that might seem strange. . . . Try again later to balance your checkbook. . . . It's okay to cry, even in front of others. . . . You can't expect to handle everything alone; ask for help. . . . Other people run out of gas, too, and they don't have your distractions. . . . It really hurts when people no longer write or call as much as they did before. . . . Put the form away until you feel more like filling it out. . . . Your son will understand that you forgot his birthday this year. . . . You will begin getting out more when you feel like it. . . . Don't expect your health to be what it was before. Just take care of yourself. . . . Pace yourself and give yourself more time to get things done. . . . You seem stronger today. . . . It's okay to be angry. Find acceptable ways to let it out. . . . Set small goals. Feel good about reaching any. . . . Nobody's perfect. Allow yourself some failures and mistakes. . . . Contain your periods of depression and feeling sorry for yourself. When the time is up, bring yourself out and get busy. . . . You did the best you could; let the guilt go. . . . What you keep calling "excuses" are actually reasons why you are feeling and behaving the way you are. Accept and understand. . . . Being late a few times is not a catastrophe. . . . Sit down and recall where you last had your keys. Retrace your steps and you will probably find them. . . . Trust yourself. You will know when it is time to reach out. . . . You have inner beauty that will show more and more. . . . It is all right for you to say that you won't accept another volunteer job. You know what you can handle. . . . You are discouraged that you are not through your grieving. Be patient. Everyone grieves in his or her own way and own time. . . . It's okay that your needs come first for now. . . . Expect some disorientation from time to time. You will come out of it. . . . You made decisions before; you will make them again. . . . It's fine to treat yourself. . . . You are a survivor. Visualize yourself as a survivor. . . . Trust yourself to do the things you need to do.

**Summary Statement:** The way I treat myself is more important than what anyone else says about me or does to me. I am with myself twenty-four hours a day. I will become more kind, loving, forgiving, supportive, and firm toward myself.

# I TALK TO MYSELF

## *Make It Nurturing*

### Some Negative Talk I've Directed toward Myself

### Nurturing Things I Need to Say

**Summary Statement:**

# GIVE UP (in Defeat) OR GIVE UP (in Release)

## *I Have a Choice*

How easy it would be to give up. Some days I do. But that feels worse than trying to go on. Is there no way out? Below, I face my defeating attitudes and attempt to release the pain that perpetuates them.

| Give Up (in Defeat) | Give Up (in Release) |
|---|---|
| I don't want to go on living without him. | I understand. Our times together held such meaning. He is gone. I let him go. My life continues. |
| I don't care what happens to me. | I let go of the claim on my life that I gave to him. I proclaim my worth, separate from him. |
| The if-only-I-hads go 'round and 'round. | Where I need forgiveness, I forgive myself. I did the best I could. |
| There is too much to manage alone. | I resent being left to handle everything. I release the resentment and get the help I need. |
| I can't bear to think about him or our times together. | I keep the beautiful memories where I can bring them out when I choose. I do not let them engulf me. |
| It was devastating the way he died. A part of me died, too. | After much retelling, I will exorcise the horrible time of his illness and death. |
| I'll never get over this. | I feel deep pain; I let it go. |
| There will never be another relationship as fulfilling. | There won't be another relationship exactly the same. I keep my heart open to the future. |

**Summary Statement:** I could give up, but I choose to go on. When the defeating times come, I will return to this page, review what I have written, and continue the process I have begun.

# GIVE UP (in Defeat) or GIVE UP (in Release)
## *I Have a Choice*

Give Up (in Defeat)                          Give Up (in Release)

**Summary Statement:**

# PROOF CALENDAR

## *Things I've Done*

Every day I record something I have done, however small. It is proof that I am functioning and in control of my life. At the end of each week, I will read all the entries for that week. The last day of the month, I'll skim the entire page and feel good about my accomplishments. Then I'll make a new calendar for the next month and keep going.

| SUNDAY | MONDAY | TUESDAY | WEDNESDAY | THURSDAY | FRIDAY | SATURDAY |
|---|---|---|---|---|---|---|
| | 1 Made some dates ahead with friends. | 2 Packed box of Joe's things to send to his son. | 3 Defrosted freezer, a job I hate. | 4 Substituted Power Bar for high fat Mexican Restaurant. | 5 Called Jan and made time to walk at her house. | 6 Relaxed and watched fun video with son. |
| 7 Weather bad. Stayed home from church and didn't feel guilty. | 8 Registered for a workshop on handling grief. | 9 "Modeled" four dresses in a style show at a luncheon. | 10 Picked up in house so it looks fairly decent all over. | 11 Curled up in front of fire. Read, slept and cried a little. | 12 Wrote difficult letter to son that I have been putting off for months. | 13 Had low fat lunch at mall with Peggy. |
| 14 Leisurely brunch with Edith after early church | 15 Wrote long letter to Joe about guilty feelings. | 16 Cleaned out clothes closet. | 17 Listed, packed clothes and put in car, ready to go to Salvation Army. | 18 Called friend whose brother just died. Listened for an hour. | 19 Splurged on a body massage. So relaxing! | 20 Went on long hike with Edith. |
| 21 Went to Singles S.S. Class for the first time. | 22 Found someone to call about heating problem. | 23 Refused delicious looking German chocolate cake at luncheon. | 24 Got car serviced, before overdue. | 25 Found some pictures of us. Cried myself to sleep. That's O.K. | 26 Worked on putting pictures in a photo album. | 27 Remembered re-cycling day. |
| 28 Visited Ralph in Rehab Center after church. | 29 Rode extra fifteen minutes on stationery bike. | 30 Made big mistake, but stopped myself from beating on me. Was understanding | 31 Fixed nice meal for myself tonight. Lit candles. | | | |

YOUR CALENDAR is on the following page. Make a number of copies before you begin. Take one copy and fill in the dates for this month. Begin recording something you do, or don't do, each day about which you feel positive. Nothing is too insignificant. Reread your calendar later and feel YOUR CONTROL over your life.

| SUNDAY | MONDAY | TUESDAY | WEDNESDAY | THURSDAY | FRIDAY | SATURDAY |
|--------|--------|---------|-----------|----------|--------|----------|
| □ | □ | □ | □ | □ | □ | □ |
| □ | □ | □ | □ | □ | □ | □ |
| □ | □ | □ | □ | □ | □ | □ |
| □ | □ | □ | □ | □ | □ | □ |
| □ | □ | □ | □ | □ | □ | □ |

# I NEED A HUG

## *It's Up to Me*

There were lots of hugs in the beginning, an acceptable way for people to show their caring. They no longer remember to do this and I miss Joe's hugs even more. I guess it is up to me. I can give a hug and get one in return. Or I can simply say, "I need a hug today."

## Little "Hugs" I Can Give Myself

BREAKFAST IN BED. The bed is still warm. And who cares if a few crumbs get scattered around when I eat my toast?

SELECTED MUSIC. Invest in some tapes of relaxing background music, with no lyrics to jar back memories.

COMFORT DRINKS. Have a variety for all through the day, ending with hot chocolate and miniature marshmallows at bedtime.

ROCKING CHAIR. I rocked my children; I'll try it for me. With the chair facing a window, I can look out and be in the sunshine.

PHONE LIFELINE. With a few selected persons, I can share all my heartaches and feel their unconditional love.

BOOKS. Old favorites are what I choose to read now. It's almost like being with a long lost friend.

AFGHAN. I like to feel the afghan my aunt made tucked tightly around me, even when I'm not cold. Her love surrounds me.

WARM BATH. I let anxieties melt away, relaxing as long as I like.

BED WARMER. Five minutes after turning the electric blanket on, my bed feels warmer and I feel more welcome there.

WORDS OF COMFORT. Reading a few verses from a book of inspirational writings brings peace at the end of my day.

HIS PILLOW. I hold his pillow and go to sleep.

**Summary Statement:** My body craves hugs. I ask for hugs from others and I give them to myself.

# I NEED A HUG

## *It's Up to Me*

My current "hug level":


Little Hugs I Can Give Myself


**Summary Statement:**

# MESSAGES TO SIGNIFICANT OTHERS

## *I Need to Say*

It was the day after the services. With utmost confidence my oldest son assured me, "Mom, I know you're strong. You're going to handle this like you've dealt with everything else in your life." I wanted to scream, "But this is different! How can I live without him?" What are the messages I need to give to my family and close friends?

OLDEST SON. I need your continued support and caring through my time of grief. Allow me to "not cope." The week you stayed after everyone else had gone meant more than I can say. Maybe the jobs you finished were done for Joe as well as for me. You loved him too. . . . How you hated to leave me home alone. Then I found the caring letter you had left. As I read it and cried, I felt your arms still around me.

MIDDLE SON. Joe's death does not mean you will have to deal with your wife's death soon. When/if that time comes, you will find the strength. Death is a fact of life and must be accepted. . . . Much of the time you hold your feelings inside. When Joe died you were able to tell me and show me how much you cared. I'm glad. Your calls have meant so much.

YOUNGEST SON. It's okay to talk about Joe's death and cry. We can do this together. Even though you are close by, I do not expect you to take Joe's place in any way. I need your help, and I appreciate your willingness, but I do not expect you to do all the work he did. I want you to feel free to move away from this area when the time is right for you. Trust me to survive when you need to go.

SISTER. It means so much to hear you say, "I pray for you every day." I do feel your prayers and your love. Being sixteen years older, you always seemed like a mother to me, and I used to resent feeling that way. In the past few years, I've come to an understanding of what your life was like and your need to be the way you are. No longer do I need to act like a rebelling teenager. I am now free to love you and provide care during your progressing illness.

CLOSE FRIEND. You came and listened for ten days! I poured out the whole story of Joe's illness and death. When I thought I was finished, I still found more. After you left, I was able to dream about Joe for the first time since his death. They were healthy dreams, a tribute to our grief work together. Thank you for listening and caring.

CLOSE FRIEND. The poems you wrote just for me I will always treasure. Almost every day I could count on a cheery postcard, a note, a call, a tiny gift from you. As I expected, messages from others dwindled to a halt. But yours have continued to the present. I know you will always be there for me.

**Summary Statement:** Putting my thoughts on paper has helped me focus on what I want to say to significant persons in my life. I will convey these messages by letter, phone, or in person.

# MESSAGES TO SIGNIFICANT OTHERS

*I Need to Say*

**Summary Statement:**

# MS. FIX-IT

## *I'm a Lone Homeowner*

Joe liked to fix things so much that I would tease him, "I believe you break things just so you can repair them!" Although I do know the difference between a Phillips screwdriver and a regular one, I never had to hold one in my hand when Joe was around. NOW what do I do? What are the basics?

## Tool Kit Kept in Special Place

Can of WD-40
Screwdrivers (regular and Phillips)
Pliers (insulated)
Assortment of screws, nuts, bolts, nails
Vice grip (small pair)
Pen flashlight with spare batteries
Electrical tape
Picture hangers
Measuring tape, ruler
Power drill

## Know Location and Operation Of:

Water shut-off valves
Electrical fuse boxes
Generator backup for furnace
Sewer system
Gas meter and line to house

## Put Dates on Calendar For:

Homeowners insurance payment
Termite control inspection
Garbage collection
Recycling pickup

## Telephone Numbers Posted

Electric company _____
Gas company _____
Water company _____
Cable company _____

Police _____
Ambulance _____
Road conditions _____
Automobile tow service _____

**Summary Statement:** My oldest son gave me the *New Complete Do-It-Yourself Manual,* by Readers Digest. I have started a service and repair file of recommended contractors. My coping philosophy is "If I can't fix it, they can." Between my own "bandaged thumb" efforts and the persons on my list, I should be able to manage.

# MS. OR MR. FIX-IT
*I'm a Lone Homeowner*

## My Lists for the Basics

**Summary Statement:**

# NEW FRIENDS

## *For My Personal Support Group*

It just happened, the special combination of three friends I've made in this first year. All are widows. Peggy's husband died two months before mine. Edith has been a widow for about two years. And Betty has passed the four-year mark.

RECENT LOSS. Peggy really does understand where I am, every day. No matter what depression or catastrophe hits, I can call this friend. She listens and knows what I am experiencing. We can spend time together, sharing or choosing not to share. We take turns crying, or cry together. There is total acceptance. It's important she is there.

TWO-YEAR-AGO LOSS. I look at Edith and think, "She's come a long way; I'll be able to do this, too." Then I hear her say, "I still can't listen to the songs that were our favorites." Remarks like this help me face the reality that my own grief process will take more than the promised one year. She still remembers much of what I'm going through but doesn't need to sink to where I am. She remains stable and up. It feels good to be with her.

OVER FOUR-YEAR-AGO LOSS. Betty talks about her husband only as part of her life history. She is so assertive and independent. I am learning much from her. We have enjoyed some trips together. Somehow knowing I can talk about my grief with her frees me from having to do so. I can safely try on my "new self without Joe" with her.

## The "How" of Making These New Friends

GROUP. After several sessions of being with Peggy in our Hospice Bereavement Group, I knew that we would have much in common. A lunch date gave us the opportunity to prove that this was true.

FRIENDS. Edith was our friends' friend. Even though she did not know us personally, Edith attended Joe's memorial service. This act of caring drew me to her and we began doing things together.

TRAVEL. A travel agent put Betty and me together for a weekend trip that we had individually chosen. We enjoyed being roommates and have since attended an Elderhostel program. Our times together are activity-oriented.

**Summary Statement:** I realize how vital it is to have friends who understand how I feel. Their being at different stages in their loss gives me perspective in my grieving process. These friends are very precious and I will keep our friendships alive. I'd like to think, however, that the next new friends I make will not be widows.

# NEW FRIENDS

*For My Personal Support Group*

## My Supportive Friends and What They Mean to Me

## Ways to Make New Friends

**Summary Statement:**

# LONELINESS IS TO BE FELT

## *Alone Time Made Better*

Friends ask, "What hurts the most?" Always I answer, "Loneliness for Joe. It never goes away." I don't want to run from this loneliness because I know to feel it is an important part of the grieving process. But my alone time can be enriched.

## Feeling My Loneliness

Don't fight it; let the feelings come. Express aloud, on paper, physically (without hurting myself), and with tears.

When feelings of loneliness for him are blocked, do something to bring on the grief: look at pictures of him and of us together, read some of his cards or letters, think about the ways I miss him, or find and hold something special that belonged to him.

Talk with others who loved him too. Cry together.

Structure my loneliness by containing it within a reasonable period of time. Then do something different. I call this "containment."

## Making Alone Time Better

Create a lovely "alone place" in my home and schedule meditation time every day. Sit for twenty minutes, completely relaxed. Say one word over and over, like "peace," "love," "one." Ignore other thoughts. Let go completely. At the end of twenty minutes, come back slowly.

Determine the time of the week that I mind being alone the most (Sundays for me). List things I might do: sit at a different place in church; take turns, with other "alone" friends, cooking and serving dinner; check television listing for special programs; drive to an area park and explore or sit and read; visit a museum; bake cookies with a borrowed kid; find a volunteer job for every Sunday.

Learn to treasure my time alone. Make a date with myself, dress up, fix a nice meal, serve it with music and candlelight. Give positive messages to myself. Stay dressed up for the rest of the evening. The next time a friend cannot go with me to something I want to attend, go alone. Consciously enjoy the moment.

**Summary Statement:** I need to differentiate between my loneliness for Joe and aloneness. Only then can I express my lonely-for-him feelings and make my alone periods more fulfilling. There are times when I now choose to be alone. In so doing, I value my own company and increase my feelings of self-worth.

# LONELINESS IS TO BE FELT

*Alone Time Made Better*


## Feeling My Loneliness


## Making Alone Time Better


**Summary Statement:**

# I'LL BE SEEING YOU

## *But I Know You Are Not There*

The man coming toward me on the street looked like Joe. I stood staring, my breath coming in little gasps. He was tall and thin. He even walked like Joe. He passed me at the corner. It certainly was not my husband. The tears came. What I wouldn't give to see Joe walking toward me again!

## Joe, I Remember You:

Coming up the steps to the deck with an armload of firewood.

Bending over the saw in your workshop.

Sitting in your chair, hands held together, fingertips touching, thinking.

Pouring batter on the griddle and flipping the pancakes.

Driving the tractor through the woods on the trails you made.

Sitting on the deck at sunset, looking out over the valley.

Driving the car, seat back as far as it would go.

Reading the most recent news magazines in bed.

Pretending you were still asleep when it was time to get up.

Putting papers in the neatly organized files in your office.

Sitting across from me at the table, reaching for my hands to hold during grace.

Cutting the loaf of bread in our favorite restaurant.

Sitting next to me in church at the end of "our" pew.

Walking the streets of the cities we visited, map in hand.

Watching the squirrel raid the bird feeder, then trying to outsmart him one more time.

**Summary Statement:** It hurts to remember you in these places, and yet it is a "good" hurt. So I will continue to remember.

# I'LL BE SEEING YOU

*But I Know You Are Not There*

When I thought that I saw you:

I Remember You:

**Summary Statement:**

# HE WASN'T PERFECT

## *No One Is*

It is difficult for me to recall things I did not like about Joe. He was so easy to live with. But, as in every relationship, there were times when we did not agree and behaviors of his that bothered me. There is a tendency, when a person dies, to forget the negatives and only remember his or her positive attributes. Joe was human and I choose to remember him that way.

## I Wish He:

Had cared more about his appearance.

Did not overreact when I asked him to do something.

Had been more sociable.

Had been freer to express negative emotions.

Could have dealt with his fear of not having sufficient savings.

Had expressed a stronger faith in God.

**Summary Statement:** I loved him just the way he was. But seeing him as he was makes grieving and letting go more possible.

## For You, the Reader

There is no way to title this exercise to fit every situation. The possibilities range from "He or she was a saint" to "I'm glad he or she is dead!" Many of us need help in working through deep anger and resentment toward the person who has died. That is beyond the scope of this book, and I trust you to get help if you need it. Whatever you do, don't skip this exercise. Choose one of the titles on the next page that best fits you, or make up your own. Doing the exercise will help you to determine if you can work on this by yourself or with a friend, or if you need professional help. Resentments held in and buried can later cause a lot of trouble.

# MY MATE WASN'T PERFECT

## *No One Is*

Use one of the following (or develop your own): "I Wish He or She," "Why Couldn't He or She," "He or She Made My Life Difficult By," "I Hated It When He or She," "I'm *Really* Angry About," "I Hated Him or Her For."

**Summary Statement:**

# I AFFIRM MYSELF

## *Again and Again*

Many times in the past, I have written affirmations for myself, putting each one on the back of a business card. Where are they? Never mind. It is better that I make new ones that affirm where I am now. Affirmations are strong and positive statements about who I am; my beliefs, strengths, and capabilities; and how I expect to be treated. They need to be as short as possible.

## My Affirmations

I, Marta, am a person of worth.
I, Marta, am unique.
I, Marta, have inner strength.
I, Marta, can cry and still be strong.
I, Marta, am a survivor.
I, Marta, value my health.
I, Marta, deserve to have my needs met.
I, Marta, have the capacity for change.
I, Marta, reach out to others.
I, Marta, have hope for the future.

## Ways of Using My Affirmations

Put each one on a separate card. Carry them in my purse to read when I have to wait somewhere.

Choose one each day to put where I can see it while I eat.

Type or write each one ten times.

Put single ones in strategic places around the house: on mirrors, in often-opened drawers, on the microwave door, and on the stove hood.

Record them and then listen to the tape in the car.

Ask a friend to read them to me, prefacing each with "You, Marta."

Sit in a relaxed position and visualize myself being the way my affirmation says I am. Visualize each affirmation in this manner.

**Summary Statement:** I will read and experience these affirmations until they are part of me. I will call them to mind throughout the day. Their truths will enable me to stand tall with my head held high. I will add more and continue to visualize each.

# I AFFIRM MYSELF

*Again and Again*

## My Affirmations

## Ways of Using My Affirmations

**Summary Statement:**

# I CARE ABOUT MY FAMILY

## *So I Put My House in Order*

With inherited longevity and good health in his favor, I expected Joe to live to be one hundred! In accepting the reality of his death, it makes me realize that I, too, am mortal.

## Things to Get Done

Update my will, to be in effect until I make a living trust.

Make an appointment with my lawyer and have him prepare:
> A durable power of attorney,
> A living will, and
> A living trust (to replace my will and avoid probate).

Make a list of my material possessions designated for certain persons.

Prepare a statement of burial wishes and suggestions for a memorial service.

Write a loving letter for each of my sons to read after my death.

Put all of the above in one of two places:

> A safety deposit box. Get an extra key and signature signing privilege for my son.

> A fire safety file. It can also hold canceled checks and income tax returns for the last three years.

Type a list entitled "What My Family Should Know"; send copies to my sons. Include names, addresses, and phone numbers of my lawyer, minister, insurance companies, broker, CPA, etc. Also include a list of important papers and where they can be found.

**Summary Statement:** Much as I dislike having to do these things, I believe each is important and needs to be done soon. I will keep this list in full sight on my desk and check off each task when completed.

# I CARE ABOUT MY FAMILY
## *So I Put My House in Order*

## Things to Get Done

**Summary Statement:**

# PUT THE CHERRY BACK ON TOP!

## *And Other Things for Me*

After months of not bothering to eat grapefruit, I sat down at breakfast with half of one in front of me. Something was missing—the cherry on the top. Always, for Joe and me, I had drizzled the halves with honey and topped them with a cherry. Am I not worth a cherry on the top? What other things am I not doing that I did before and I still deserve?

## I Deserve To:

Comb my hair and put on lipstick first thing every day.

Start making my bed again.

Make brewed coffee instead of instant to start my day.

Go for a drive on a pretty day. Discover a new restaurant or store.

Make pancakes, just for me.

Give myself nice presents at Christmas, Valentine's Day, and my birthday.

Look for a new recipe, fix it for me, and freeze leftovers in individual portions.

Make dinner alone special. Freshen my makeup. Change clothes for my TV dinner date with my favorite news commentator.

Buy a new article of clothing in a bright color.

Treat myself to a manicure or pedicure.

Take myself out to eat at a nice restaurant. Read a book or "people watch."

Program a relaxing bath: bubbles, music, candlelight.

**Summary Statement:** I am special and I deserve any of these things I choose to do for me. I will look for more special treats.

# PUT THE CHERRY BACK ON TOP!
## *And Other Things for Me*

When and how have I been denying that I am special?


## I Deserve To:


**Summary Statement:**

# THAT MAGIC MOMENT

## *The Story of How We Met*

Tiny incidents from that evening are etched in my memory. I know what I was wearing: black slacks and a tapestry jacket. The jacket still hangs in the back of my closet, having gone in and out of style many times. I like to recall that time.

One enchanted evening, I noticed a stranger across a crowded room. The setting was a birthday party for my best friend. Most of the people I knew, but who was that tall man across the room? He was eating peanuts like he had just discovered them! At that moment he glanced up and our eyes met and held. When I could disentangle myself from the group I was with, I made my way to where he stood. He didn't say hello but simply offered me peanuts! Little did I know that he would always share what he enjoyed with me, for the rest of our lives together.

We didn't begin with chit-chat as most people do, but at a deeper level: our relationship with our grown children, the world situation, and many other things. Finally, we got around to "I'm Joe" and "I'm Marta."

The friends I had come with were leaving early to go to another party. What stroke of fate kept me from going with them? "I'll stay and take a taxi home," I said.

Later that evening, Joe and I found ourselves together again. This time it felt like we were old friends, and we picked up where we had left off. We had so much to say to each other. When he asked me to go to dinner with him, I agreed with no hesitation. At that time in my life, such a response was totally out of character. I learned later that Joe's even being at the party was unusual for him.

As we walked to the place where I could catch a taxi, he lightly put his arm about my shoulder and helped me around some obstacles. My eyes filled with tears, remembering some past hurts. In that moment I knew that here was a man who would protect and help me, and my intuition proved true.

**Summary Statement:** It feels good to relive that evening. I am thankful that, against so many odds, we were able to meet. We sensed that there could be something special between us, and we made it happen!

# THAT MAGIC MOMENT

*The Story of How We Met*

**Summary Statement:**

# THE GUILT TRIP GOES ON

## *Unless I End It*

I've heard myself saying, "One thing I'm thankful for is that I have no regrets." That isn't entirely true. When I look deep enough, I find those guilty feelings that were there all the time.

| What I Feel Guilty About | Ending It |
|---|---|
| Not fulfilling the one request he made in the hospital. | Hear him saying (if he could), "Marta, it's okay." Accept it. |
| Not talking with him about his death when it became inevitable. | Somehow I felt that talking about it would make it real, and I could not deal with that. Understand; forgive myself. |
| Spending so much of our time together talking about my needs and activities. | He was the silent type. Acknowledge only the guilt I'm due, then let it go. |
| Planning so many trips the year before he became ill. There were jobs he wanted to do at home. | He enjoyed our trips. Let myself mourn his unfulfilled dreams. |
| Giving him gifts I wanted him to have and so few that I knew he wanted. | You're only human. Forgive your failings. Remember the gifts he loved. |
| Taking personally our big discussion about finances. He got upset and I struck back. | I now understand why we each reacted as we did. I forgive myself for the way I handled my part. |

**Summary Statement:** In these situations guilt serves no purpose. It gets me stuck in my grieving process. I need to recognize guilt, check its validity, forgive where needed, and be sure I let it go.

# THE GUILT TRIP GOES ON
## *Unless I End It*

**What I Feel Guilty About**                    **Ending It**

**Summary Statement:**

# WHO TAKES CARE OF ME?

## *I Do*

The loss of a spouse puts me at the **very top** of the Stress Factor List. What if I get sick? There's no one to say, "Let me tuck you in bed and bring you some chicken soup." I feel physically, mentally, and emotionally drained. That scares me. I'm a prime target for a health hazard. If ever I needed to observe basic health care, it is NOW.

## Every Day I Promise Myself That I Will:

KEEP TO A REGULAR SLEEP SCHEDULE, whether I sleep solidly or not. I will limit my sleeping pills to the early weeks of my grieving period.

EXERCISE, doing something I enjoy. Include a friend whenever I can.

EAT RIGHT, which means lots of fruits, vegetables (raw is fine), and whole-grain breads and cereals. Stick to nonfat or low-fat dairy products. Avoid alcohol and caffeine in any form.

EXPRESS FEELINGS through crying, journal writing, talking with family and friends, or physical outlets.

NURTURE MYSELF with loving and caring messages all through the day. Watch out for put-downs and negatives. "Tape" positives on top.

MEDITATE/PRAY, working toward ten to twenty minutes twice a day. Consider deep breathing exercises, repeating a favorite word, and other relaxation techniques.

## Later I Promise Myself To:

Tailor a stress release program to my needs.

Keep a "Talk to Doctor" file. Include notes and articles to share.

Expand my exercise program. Include variety, especially a weight-bearing exercise.

Be aware if I am eating to fill the void or not eating because I am lonely.

Establish new eating places and patterns.

Take vitamin, mineral, and calcium supplements if needed, but no megadoses. Take vitamin B6, the "stress vitamin," throughout this first year.

Check my weight once a week. Keep within the recommended range through exercise and a healthy eating program.

Drink six to eight glasses of water per day. Keep a filled water pitcher on the counter as a reminder.

Find a buddy and remind each other of monthly breast self-examinations.

Put reminders of appointments on a calendar: dental, eye exam, physical, and mammogram.

Be careful around steps, slippery areas (shower, tub), kitchen knives.

Read *Prevention* or *Health* magazine.

Find a volunteer job that makes me feel fulfilled.

Cultivate healthy-minded friends. Compare notes; share what's new.

**Summary Statement:** I will make a "Have you . . ." card with the six areas listed. This will go where I can see it as a daily reminder. Later I will work on the longer list, checking off as I go. Taking care of my health is the most important thing I can do for myself.

# WHO TAKES CARE OF ME?
*I Do*

Every Day I Promise Myself That I Will:

Later I Promise Myself To:

**Summary Statement:**

# DEAR JOE, IT'S ME, MARTA

## *Letters Not to Be Mailed*

Joe made a small request while he was in the hospital that I did not fulfill. After he died, I recalled this incident. For days I wallowed in remorse for not having done what he had asked. It was as if I needed something to feel guilty about. Nothing I did made me feel any better. In desperation, I grabbed my legal pad and started writing a letter to him, pouring out my heart. After pages of "talking" to him, I felt relief. Many letters have been written since then, prefaced with "I know you're not going to get this, but I need to talk to you."

## Excerpts from My Letters to Joe

. . . I'm so thankful you don't know about the family problems. You'd be hurting, too. But here I can tell you. . . . Is it possible that, wherever you are, you are aware of only the good things happening to me? I believe that is true. I also see you being healthy and happy.

. . . Edith and I saw *Nunsense* today at the dinner theater where you and I used to go. I haven't laughed that hard since you've been gone. It was such a release! Now I'm having different feelings. I feel guilty that I had so much fun without you. I didn't even think about you during the play. Isn't it silly for me to feel that way? You, of all people, would want me to enjoy life. I hope I can remember that.

. . . I'm so frustrated and upset! The carpenter was here today. The questions are endless! What had you planned to do with. . . ? Where did you put. . . ? What should I do in this situation. . . ? And that? Where do I get. . . ? If you were here you would know the answers. As I write this, I realize why I'm resenting Jim's presence so intensely. He represents your dying and not being able to do these things, and my inadequacies. How can I blame you for dying? So I'm blaming Jim and myself. Now I understand.

. . . You will find it hard to believe this. I'm taking a wood carving class! It's the last thing you would expect me to do. You'd love it and do a super job. Is that why I enrolled? Tonight was the first class and I cut my thumb. You know how great I am with tools! But you can tell that my wooden mouse is a mouse!

. . . Sometimes I've looked forward to today, the one-year anniversary of your death. When the going was rough this year, I'd say to myself what I had heard so many times, "The first year is the hardest." So here I am on January 25, and it still hurts! It's not over. But I have survived. I've let myself grieve and I've taken control of my life. Those were my only goals this year. I can hear you say, "You've done well, kid. I'm proud of you." I feel proud of me, too.

**Summary Statement:** My letters to Joe provide a special kind of release. There are also times when reading them again is just what I need to do.

# Letter Not to Be Mailed

Date _____

Dear _____, It's me, _____

**Summary Statement:**

# MAKE MY HOME MINE

### *I'm the One Who Must Live Here*

It is in the bedroom where I miss Joe the most. If I make some changes, especially in the area I can see from the bed, maybe it will be easier to be there.

| Situation | Plan for Change |
|---|---|
| Bedroom with most of the furnishings built in. | Put bench along wall. Add artificial tree. |
| No seating in kitchen. I refuse to face his empty chair in the dining area. | Get bar stools and eat at island in kitchen. Look out window. |
| His office in the house, with no one using it. | Donate his books. Empty desk drawers. Adapt his files for me. |
| His garage work area in disarray. | Put Joe's special tools out of sight. Organize what I expect to use. |
| Bird feeder a delight, but requires daily refilling. | Purchase a bird feeder with much larger capacity. |
| Steps to deck often icy in winter; dangerous getting firewood. | Construct readily accessible wood storage unit just outside door. |
| Poor lighting where I've chosen to sit in living room. | Find lamp that will furnish adequate lighting. |

**Summary Statement:** Nothing will bring him back, but I have a life to live. I need not feel guilty, as I had been, about making changes. It is with pride that I work within my home to make it more livable and enjoyable for me.

# MAKE MY HOME MINE

*I'm the One Who Must Live Here*

Feelings I have about making changes in my home:

Situation                                   Plan For Change

Summary Statement:

# LOOKING GOOD

## *Putting My Best Face Forward*

For a long time after Joe's death, I did not care how I looked. It was a matter of survival, one day at a time. Before, I had enjoyed making myself attractive, mostly for me. What about now?

## Ideas for Improving My Appearance

Get a new hairstyle, with regular trims. Consider highlighting or coloring.

Have a makeover done at a department store. Will get ideas and don't have to buy.

Take to Salvation Army my drab, dull clothes that do nothing for me. Buy a few clothes in happy colors that light me up. Include one outfit for special occasions.

Sew stylish new buttons on tired but still good jacket. Resurrect other pieces of clothing.

Treat myself to a manicure and new polish.

Sample perfume sprays and select one that fits me.

Make a pact with a friend who also needs to lose weight and get rid of these ten extra pounds.

Replace my worn-out exercise clothes with an attractive new outfit.

Choose a new pair of earrings in a style I've never worn before.

Tilt the car mirror up slightly, forcing me to sit tall.

**Summary Statement:** My self-worth is not to be measured by my appearance. As I am feeling better on the inside, however, I want my appearance to match that. I choose to become more attractive. This is a neat list of fun things to do.

# LOOKING GOOD

*Putting My Best Face Forward*

**How I feel about how I look:**

## Ideas for Improving My Appearance

**Summary Statement:**

# A DECISION I NEED TO MAKE

## *Keep Francis; Let Francis Go*

Five weeks after Joe's death, my car was totaled. Thankfully, no one was seriously injured. So I have been driving "Francis," our second car, full time. Francis is a '67 Dynamic Olds 88 we purchased for $300 six years ago. We fell in love with Francis and had him put in mint condition. (It was "Frances" when Joe drove it—he favored girl cars—and "Francis" when I was behind the wheel.) Francis performed beautifully on two long trips. But I don't need two cars. Should I get rid of Francis and purchase a new car? I choke up at the thought!

### Pro (Keep Francis)

Heavy car; I feel safer
Insurance cost is low
Low maintenance and upkeep
White is a "safe" color
Excellent mechanic available
Great mechanical shape
Huge trunk for hauling
Beautiful, long classic lines
Solid ride; holds the road
Body in great shape; no rust or rattles
Paid for; no car payments
Probably safe from carjackers
Great sentimental attachment

### Con (Let Francis Go)

Guzzles gas; low gas mileage
Doesn't have front-wheel drive
Heater doesn't work well
Requires large parking space
Needs big area to turn around
AM radio only

## Other Decisions Ahead of Me

Stay in this home or move to a smaller one.
Remain in this area or move closer to my family.
Go back to school or not.
Find a job or do volunteer work.
Stay in my chosen field or try something new.
Take a trip next year.
Get professional help with investments or do it on my own.

**Summary Statement:** I have decided that Francis will live, at least for now. I will have an FM radio and cassette player installed and ride in style! This pro and con decision-making process can be used for other decisions as well.

# A DECISION I NEED TO MAKE

My decision and why I need to make it:

Pro                                                    Con

Other Decisions Ahead of Me

**Summary Statement:**

# MEMORIALS

## *For Memories and Tributes*

I want to remember Joe and the life and love we shared. I also will create memorials as tributes to the life he lived.

| Memorials to Joe | Their Meaning for Me |
|---|---|
| Plant a pink dogwood tree where I can see it from the kitchen. It will bloom in the early spring. | Spring was his favorite season. Pink dogwood is special to me, as he was. |
| Have a heart made from his wedding band. Wear it on a chain under my clothes. | His heart will be next to mine, where I can feel it all the time. |
| Donate books to the library in his memory. | He loved to read for education and for fun. |
| Sort through our photos. Make albums of his life and our time together. | He lived a full and happy life. Here is the proof. |
| Volunteer to help serve food on Thanksgiving and Christmas at the Salvation Army. | The Salvation Army was Joe's favorite charity. |
| Contribute to a scholarship fund in his name. | Young people will receive help to go forward with their lives. |

**Summary Statement:** As I pay tribute to him through these memorials, I feel closer to him, and his life continues.

# MEMORIALS
*For Memories and Tributes*

Memorials to _____                    **Their Meaning for Me**

**Summary Statement:**

# A BREAK IN THE CLOUDS

## *That I Create*

In that fuzzy time, when my eyes were still shut but I knew that it was morning, I realized that I did not want to open my eyes and face the day. How much easier it would be just to drift back to sleep and pretend IT never happened. No. TODAY I will create a little happiness for myself.

## Something to Look Forward To

Tie a yellow ribbon on a pretty basket. Fill it with cards and letters that offer comfort. Read and reread them as needed throughout the day.

Memorize an inspirational quote, such as a Bible verse, and repeat it to myself all through the day.

Put on rain gear and walk with the light rain on my face.

Gather flowers and place them in small containers around the house.

Call one of my best friends for no reason except to stay in touch.

Simmer whole cloves and cinnamon in a saucepan. Let the memories come: mother's apple pie, special Christmas cookies, and red hot candies.

Have music tapes ready for periods of cleaning, mealtime, and relaxing.

Make a small purchase, maybe a magazine or scented candle. Use it as a reward for getting some thing difficult finished.

Sit with a travel brochure and dream about taking a trip.

Borrow a book or audiocassette book from the library.

Discover a new flavored coffee or herb tea.

Find a seed catalog and pick out bulbs to plant.

Send a picture postcard of my area to invite a friend for a visit.

Rent a light video and have popcorn ready to munch while I watch it.

Select an exotic fruit and plan when to have it as a treat.

Send a tiny, secret gift to someone I love.

Make a luncheon date and put it on my calendar.

Celebrate the first leaf to fall in autumn, the first snowflake of winter, and bring in a small branch with buds in the early spring.

**Summary Statement:** Small treats can help make long days bearable. I will plan something special every day, look forward to it, savor it, and gain strength for facing the rest of the day.

# A BREAK IN THE CLOUDS

## *That I Create*

### Something to Look Forward To

**Summary Statement:**

# MY MEMORY QUILT

*It Keeps Me Warm*

The dozen red roses from you.

Riding the ferris wheel and having our pictures taken.

The day the pigeon pooped on my face.

When the minister was late for our wedding

You worked hard to let my son beat you at pool.

Our "Charlie Brown" first Christmas tree and how we loved it.

The many times you had tears in your eyes. You were not ashamed to cry.

Our 29 mile bicycle ride.

Your deep belly laughs.

How we pretended we didn't know each other, met in a hotel and spent the night. You were cool!

Your need to cuddle, and the teddy bear I always left on your pillow when I had to be away.

The last words you said, "I love you."

The fun you had playing with children.

Your china-blue eyes.

**Summary Statement:** I snuggle under this quilt and feel loved and secure. It is always here where I can touch the feelings I had then. It makes me smile, remembering Joe and our years together.

# MY MEMORY QUILT

*It Keeps Me Warm*

**Summary Statement:**

# THAT CAN'T BE ME

## *That Person Is Old!*

Recently I was leafing through my son's photo album. Seeing a picture of an older woman I did not recognize, I asked, "Who is that?" He replied, "Why, Mom, that's you." It had been taken after Joe's death. There was no denying, the woman in that photo was haggard and looked old. I feel I have lost a youthful part of me, and I understand why. I'd like to bring it back.

| What I've Lost | How to Regain It |
| --- | --- |
| Stamina | Begin by walking three times a week. Use a stationary bike on other days or when it rains. Try a yoga tape. Work toward a balanced combination. |
| My excitement over little things | Focus on at least one beautiful thing each day. Really taste every morsel of a favorite food, like a slice of bread. |
| The bounce in my step | Wear a rubber band on my wrist as a reminder to walk with a purpose. |
| My smile | Encourage myself to smile at everyone I meet. |
| Good posture (walking and sitting tall) | Do mental and mirror checks throughout the day. |
| Laughter | Start reading the comics. Collect jokes to share with friends. Read books by Erma Bombeck, George Burns, and other humorists. Watch funny videos and TV shows. |
| A reason for living | Make a list of short-term and long-term goals. Outline some plans. Share them with a partner; inspire each other. |

**Summary Statement:** I'm on my way. Each little step helps, onward and upward.

# THAT CAN'T BE ME

## *That Person Is Old!*

**How old do I feel?** If someone took a picture of me or I looked in a mirror, how old would I say that person was? Is that older than I really am?

| What I've Lost | How to Regain It |
|---|---|
| | |

**Summary Statement:**

# I NEED TO GO BACK

## *To Where It Happened*

I sat in the car, unable to put my hand on the door handle to open it. Joe's nephew said, "You don't have to go in; you can change your mind." But I knew I had to go into the Houston hospital where Joe had died. The five weeks we spent there had been so terrible that I had blocked them from my mind. I needed to make that experience real before I could let it go.

## Where I Need to Go and What I Need to Do

HOSPITAL WHERE HE DIED. Walk the hall to "our" room. Go in if I can. Relive the experience. Say my good-byes to Joe again. Make my circuit walk around the halls. Visit the chapel and pray. Talk to the nurses who were there when we were. Go out the front door and leave his "dying time" behind.

OUR FIRST HOME. Walk along the street. Take pictures. Sit on a bench and remember. Go to our church. Visit the library. Spend time with our favorite neighbor who still lives next door. Walk the aisles in our supermarket. Eat at the corner restaurant. Remember, treasure, and release the past.

WHERE WE LIVED MOST OF OUR MARRIED LIFE. Call a friend in that area and make arrangements to stay with her. Set a luncheon date and invite all the friends who still live there. Talk about Joe and the times we spent together. Take the same early morning walk we always took. Visit his workplace and mine. Eat at the very special restaurant we always called "ours." Drink a toast to Joe. Devote one day to making a video of our life there. Take with me when I leave what I want to remember, always conscious that it belongs to yesterday.

**Summary Statement:** These pilgrimages are so painful, but necessary. I trust myself that in each place I will know what I need to do. I will allow plenty of time to recall, to feel, to grieve, and then to let go. In letting go of the past, I make room for the future.

# I NEED TO GO BACK
## *To Where It Happened*

### Where I Need to Go and What I Need to Do

**Summary Statement:**

# I BELIEVE IN ME

## *My Positive Traits Are Still There*

"You are so well organized," everyone used to tell me. Admittedly, that was true. But if ever there was a time when I needed to bring structure into my life, it is now. I would feel more secure and in control. Also, I must have other attributes that I can rely on.

## Positive Attributes I Can Think Of

| | | |
|---|---|---|
| friendly | cheerful | curious |
| organized | attractive | outgoing |
| humorous | caring | serene |
| resourceful | thoughtful | healthy |
| determined | creative | sympathetic |
| worthwhile | understanding | capable |
| hardworking | independent | giving |
| gentle | sincere | aesthetic |
| quiet | dependable | forgiving |
| courageous | optimistic | contented |
| confident | tenacious | assertive |
| intelligent | vivacious | cooperative |
| tolerant | motivated | kind |
| insightful | helpful | resilient |
| tender | religious | honest |
| realistic | open | honorable |
| courageous | worthwhile | humble |

I will underline characteristics that I have and copy them on a card:

## I Am:

ORGANIZED
CREATIVE
UNDERSTANDING
MOTIVATED
FORGIVING

**Summary Statement:** As I look at my card each day, I will think of ways to use these strengths. I will visualize myself being that way.

# I BELIEVE IN ME

## *My Positive Traits Are Still There*

**My Positive Traits**                    **How I Can Use Them Now**

**Summary Statement:**

# PUT TO GOOD USE

## *When I Am Ready*

In the beginning, if I started to move Joe's things, I felt like I was getting rid of him. Slowly, I was able to pack away some of his items and make more room for mine. They went into drawers and an empty closet. "I'll take care of them some day." For me, that day is here.

| Items | Possible Use |
|---|---|
| Blood pressure machine | *Donate it to the medical clinic. |
| His work coat | Wear it myself when I carry in wood and fill the bird feeders. |
| Technical books | *Donate them to the university. |
| Mustache trimming set | Offer it to son who has a mustache. |
| Pocket knife from Bangkok | Give it to son who especially loved to hear about Joe's travels. |
| Several pairs of eyeglasses | Donate them at eye clinic. |
| Favorite red suede vest | Have it altered to fit me. |
| Carpentry tools | Give them to son who is remodeling home. |
| London Fog raincoat | Give it to Joe's nephew who wears same size. |
| Magazines | Drop them off at library. |
| Leftover clothes | *Donate them to Salvation Army. |
| Tiny pocket comb he always carried | Keep it in the bottom of my purse, where I can touch it anytime. |
| Electric razor | Offer it to son who gave it to him. |
| The rest of his personal things that I want to keep | Place them lovingly in a cedar chest. Look at them whenever I choose. |

*Obtain donation statement for income taxes.

**Summary Statement:** For me, it has been helpful to wait to disperse Joe's belongings. I can make wiser decisions now and choose people who will appreciate his belongings. His memory lives on in the things he used.

# PUT TO GOOD USE

*When I Am Ready*

**My feelings about dealing with my mate's belongings:**

| Remaining Items | Possible Use |
| --- | --- |

**Summary Statement:**

# TO BE LIKE JOE

## *I'm Free to Choose*

Joe had offered to make a file cabinet for me, indicating that he would begin that day. After seeing him sitting in his favorite chair for a long time and seemingly doing nothing, I asked, "What happened to the file project?" "I'm working on it," he replied.

## Lessons I Learned from Joe

Thinking and planning time are as important as working time.

Don't sweat the little things.
Most problems are just that.
Save your time and energy for the big ones.

Travel, to be appreciated fully, must be done leisurely.
Adventure on foot whenever possible.

Select one task at a time.
Follow it through to completion and do it well.

Accept people as they are.
They are doing the best they can for now.

Also accept yourself.
Forgive your mistakes.
Savor your successes.

**Summary Statement:** These were words of wisdom that Joe lived by and that I admire. I choose to make them part of my life. In so doing, Joe's principles live on.

# TO BE LIKE _____

*I'm Free to Choose*


**Lessons I Learned from** _____


**Summary Statement:**

# SO LET US CELEBRATE!

## *I Count My Blessings*

Every Sunday morning our minister starts the service with an introductory phrase followed by, "So let us celebrate!" During the week, when there was something for which Joe was thankful, he would often say, "So let us celebrate," exactly mimicking the minister's voice and intonations. It always made me smile. I realize I have not been celebrating my blessings.

## I Celebrate My:

Family who loves me

Two best friends, and other friends

"Talking" relationship with God

Church and worship that spiritually fulfill me

Five senses in good working order

Home where I feel secure

Returning appetite and good health

Project that gives purpose to my life

Trusted renter in my apartment

Finances sufficient for my needs

Treasured memories of my time with Joe

Beginnings of a new life

**Summary Statement:** My many blessings have gotten drowned in my sorrows. Here I lift them out, one by one. I will list more. I need to read this list often and realize how truly blessed I am.

# SO LET US CELEBRATE!

*I Count My Blessings*

**Summary Statement:**

# TIME GOES BY

## *Nothing Gets Done*

In the early months after Joe's death, I was unaware—nor would I have cared—that things were piling up. Grieving was all-consuming. Now, however, my productive nature is beginning to surface. I am increasingly frustrated as the days float by and nothing seems to be accomplished. What happens to my time?

| Time Wasters | Time Savers |
|---|---|
| Reading newspapers, catalogs, and junk mail. | Use TV or mealtime to skim these. |
| Jumping from one task to another. | Train myself to finish one task before starting another. |
| Moving in slow motion. | Enjoy a small reward on completion of each task. |
| Allowing phone calls to take too much time. | Consolidate calls. Stick to the topic. Do body exercises while on the phone. |
| Putting off jobs I don't like and letting them pile up. | Make a list each day, rank the jobs, and check them off as they're completed. |
| Spending hours watching news and reading news magazines. | Use TV and radio news time to get other things done. Skim magazines. |
| Making numerous trips into town, taking longer than expected. | Keep a running list of errands to do in one trip. |
| Looking at everything that needs to be done and giving up in despair. | Take one day at a time. At the end of each day, take pride in finished tasks. Begin with a new plan the next day. |

**Summary Statement:** These are better ways of making use of my time. I'll work while I work, play when I play, and find both fulfilling.

# TIME GOES BY

*Nothing Gets Done*

My time management assessment:

Time Wasters                                             Time Savers

**Summary Statement:**

# THE THREE-LETTER WORD

## *What about Sex?*

I am a sexual being. Why is there no exercise in my spiral notebooks designed to deal with sex? Because when Joe died I chose to push it aside and pretend that part of me did not exist. That is not fair to me. Nor is it being true to our beautiful sexual relationship. I did not die when Joe did. But what can I do?

STOP RUNNING. Don't look away when there are tender love scenes on TV or in movies. Watch and let myself feel, even if it hurts terribly. Read, instead of skipping over, those intimate parts in books. Bring back into focus couples holding hands and smiling at each other. Let myself see men as men again.

KEEP ALIVE PHYSICALLY. I had no qualms about pleasuring myself during long absences from Joe or when health prevented sexual intercourse. The first time I tried after his death, however, I couldn't continue. I curled up in a ball and sobbed, missing him and the sexual fulfillment we knew. To keep juices flowing and prevent atrophy of my sexual being, I need to continue this avenue of release.

FEEL SEXUAL. Sexuality in the broader sense means I can feel like a woman without a sexual partner. I choose to look attractive and move in graceful ways, not as a come-on for men, but as a reflection of the real me. I *am* a woman.

BE WILLING TO RISK. There may be a close relationship in my future. Up to now I've rejected it, saying I don't want it. I am becoming a whole person. I am free to choose. There is no need to rush to fill the void or sublimate what is lost. I can take my time and move from friendship to respect and then to trust, if it is right for me. A new relationship will be different from what I have known. If it is not to be, I can handle that, too.

**Summary Statement:** Becoming more sexually alive is being true to myself and to my love life with Joe. I will "tend" this part of me. I remain open to experiencing new intimacies, while keeping the woman in me alive.

# THE THREE-LETTER WORD
*What about Sex?*

**Where am I sexually?**

## What I Need to Do

**Summary Statement:**

# IT WAS A COMFORT
## *When They Reached Out*

I remember with such affection the loving things some people did and said. I continue to feel loved, just remembering.

## Listening

In the beginning, my greatest need was just to talk. It helped when I felt certain people really wanted to hear what I needed to say. I saw acceptance in their eyes. They did not interrupt and seemed comfortable when I said nothing or just cried. They held my hand. No advice was given. They listened as long as I needed to talk.

## Words

"It's okay. I'm still listening. I have lots of time." "I always admired Joe. He was my mentor. Much of what he taught me has stayed with me." "I remember the love in Joe's eyes when he talked about you." "In all the many years I knew Joe, I never heard him say a critical word about another person." "I don't know how you feel, but if you want to talk, I'll listen." "I have been thinking about you and wanted to call and tell you that I care." "I'm hurting, not like you, but I miss him, too." "I'll just be here beside you." "Let the tears come; I don't mind." "I love you."

## Deeds

A friend called long distance every evening at 9:30 for the first ten days I was alone. "I'm just calling to hear about your day and to tuck you into bed." There were notes, sometimes short, that continued long after most people stopped writing; food, in disposable pans, that could be frozen and used later; a specific invitation to lunch or dinner. A visitor brought a box of new herbal tea. "I'm going grocery shopping. Want to come along?" A Peace plant was sent to my home with a loving note. A touch on the arm, squeeze of the hand, or a full-fledged hug were given naturally and sincerely. "Let's plan to spend the day together on your anniversary. I'll think of things for us to do." Letters and calls were received long after his death.

**Summary Statement:** As I write the above, I remember how good each contact felt and the comfort it brought. With these in mind, I can choose more wisely what to do for others when they are hurting.

# IT WAS A COMFORT
## *When They Reached Out*

Listening

Words

Deeds

**Summary Statement:**

# WIDOWED, MARRIED, OR SINGLE

## *Where Am I Now?*

The form had only two places to check: "Married" or "Single." There was no "Widowed" to hide behind. I hate that word anyway. So what am I, married or single? Or do I write in "widow"?

WIDOW. That's not me. A widow is dressed in black, with a matching black veil. She walks slowly, alone, following the casket to the grave in the rain. She never smiles and talks constantly about her husband and cries all the time. How awful! How did I get that picture so fixed in my mind? No wonder I refuse to label myself "widow."

MARRIED. Legally, I am no longer married. But I can still write "Mrs." before my name and use his last name as mine. I wear the wedding band he gave me. Doesn't that make me married? I feel married. Am I clinging to the married state because I cannot face the reality of his death? That would make sense.

SINGLE. This sounds even worse! It brings to mind desperately lonely people reaching out to other lonely people in bars and singles' clubs. It could mean dating and all that. That's not for me.

## Checking Out and Moving between States

WIDOW. I never wear black; it's not my color. I now consciously choose bright colors that look good on me. I don't have to talk about Joe all the time. I still get tears in my eyes, but not at every reminder of him. Often I write my name as Marta Felber and it looks okay. I've thought about a time in the future when I will take off my ring.

MARRIED. I want to feel married because that makes Joe seem closer. I don't want to lose him. The reality I must face is that he is dead. Our marriage in the here and now no longer exists. That hurts terribly, but I need to let it go. Ours was a good marriage, but it is over.

SINGLE. I can be single and not be looking for another relationship. I can begin to operate from the state of singleness with strength. This means I am my own person, unique. I do not have to depend on someone else for who I am. I am me.

**Summary Statement:** Except on legal forms, I am free to choose what I am. It's okay to see myself as either married, widowed, or single. I believe I am in transition, moving between these states, becoming an independent single. That's okay, too.

# WIDOWED, MARRIED, OR SINGLE
## *Where Am I Now?*

How I feel about being:

### Widowed

### Married

### Single

**Summary Statement:**

# THE YO-YO YEAR

## *It's Been Up and Down*

What an appropriate image! A yo-yo goes up and down, down and up. That is exactly how my year has gone.

UP: Held up really well during his death and services.
   DOWN: Fell apart ten days later when everyone left.

DOWN: "I don't want to live without him," I said over and over.
   UP: "But I don't want to die, and I won't."

UP: Appreciated my first trip away from home.
   DOWN: I was devastated on return; he wasn't there!

DOWN: I was hit with two huge expenditures I had not expected.
   UP: Took a quick look at finances and decided I could manage.

UP: There were promises of an easy and early estate settlement.
   DOWN: There were complications, with probate dragging on and on.

UP: Spent seven fulfilling days in San Francisco with a friend.
   DOWN: I was confined to bed with a sinus infection on return.

DOWN: Had six disasters within a few days.
   UP: Then had a calm period for a couple of weeks.

UP: Sang happy birthday to our two-year-old twin granddaughters.
   DOWN: Realized Joe won't see them grow up.

UP: Survived Christmas better than I thought I would.
   DOWN: Sunk to a deep depression on New Year's Day.

**Summary Statement:** This has been a rough year with many ups and downs. I feel good that I have survived as well as I have. Life will begin to level off. I am sure of that.

# THE YO-YO YEAR
### *It's Been Up and Down*

## My Specific Yo-Yo Times

**Summary Statement:**

# IT WILL GET BETTER

## *That's What Everyone Said*

Everyone I talked to made this promise. In the beginning I resented hearing over and over, "It will get better." At that point I couldn't focus on the future, only on the tremendous pain of the present. Nearing the end of my first year of grieving, I realize that all those persons were right. It is getting better.

## It Is Getting Better—How I Know

### I Compare NOW with BEFORE

NOW I don't cry as much. BEFORE, a song, sight, thought, ad, or item in the grocery store would trigger tears.

NOW I dream about him less often. When I do, the dreams are about times we enjoyed. BEFORE, the dreams were often of his illness and death.

NOW I don't feel I have to talk about him all the time. BEFORE, I needed to tell everyone I met, "My husband died."

NOW I can think more clearly, I can focus on a problem, and I am less forgetful. BEFORE, I was constantly confused, forgetting to do important things, and driving to the wrong place.

NOW my weight is almost normal. BEFORE, I was underweight, then overweight.

NOW I'm sleeping through most nights. BEFORE, I had trouble getting to sleep, then I would wake at 2:00 or 4:00 A.M. and be unable to get back to sleep.

NOW I am reaching out to others in need. BEFORE, I was totally submerged in my own loss.

NOW I can begin to think about goals, short term and long range. BEFORE, I felt it didn't matter what happened to the rest of my life.

NOW I find myself laughing spontaneously. I'm smiling again. BEFORE, every laugh was forced and I felt my face would crack.

**Summary Statement:** My days have gotten better and will continue to do so. I need to stop from time to time and acknowledge these positive changes. Then I can move in the direction of claiming my new life.

# IT WILL GET BETTER

*That's What Everyone Said*

How I felt when people said, "It will get better":

## It Is Getting Better - How I Know

### I Compare NOW with BEFORE

**Summary Statement:**

# GOOD-BYES ARE HARD TO SAY

## *But the Time Has Come*

Good-byes are necessary and even healthy. They provide closure and complete unfinished business. The time has come for me to remember and say good-bye to my life with Joe, our hopes, and our dreams.

## I Need to Say Good-Bye To:

New things we had planned to learn together: computer literacy, "throwing" a pot, Elderhostel programs, acting workshops, courses at the university, lessons for South American dancing, or bird watching and identification of bird calls. I may do some of these things, but it is good-bye to our sharing these experiences.

Our "dates," taking each other out to eat. The one being taken did not know the destination, adding suspense. It was a neat thing to do and we did it for years. But it will be no more for us. Good-bye.

The best traveling companion I ever had. He taught me to "hang loose." Before I met him, I had to do every touristy thing. "If you run yourself ragged from morning to night, you won't remember a thing. You'll be exhausted," he claimed. "We'll choose a couple of things each day that we really want to see or do and then relax." How wise he was. Good-bye to my best traveling companion.

Using each other as sounding boards when we had concerns and problems related to family members. He was the only one who really understood. I say good-bye to my "special listener."

Growing old together. Somehow I did not dread those advancing years, knowing we would be in it together. I was confident that we would poke fun at our aches and pains, exercise together, and eat healthy. Joe would have mellowed with age; he was that type. I let my "ageless" partner go.

The lover who shared my bed, his body that I could touch and feel, the many hugs, and closeness. Good-bye to all those intimate times.

**Summary Statement:** The memories I can keep forever. I say good-bye to his actual presence. I let him go.

# GOOD-BYES ARE HARD TO SAY

## *But the Time Has Come*

**I Need to Say Good-bye To:**

**Summary Statement:**

# NEW YEAR'S DAY

## *Can Be Any Day*

Last January 1 was a complete washout! I allowed a disturbing telephone conversation with a family member to push me into deep depression. Any thoughts of evaluating my past year and making resolutions were abandoned. So I've chosen TODAY as my New Year's Day instead. I take stock of my life.

WHERE HAVE I BEEN? I've been to the bottom! Those periods of deep mourning for Joe were the absolute pits. I went through it, as I knew I had to, but thank God the worst is over. I've dealt with frustrations, disappointments, and loneliness. I'm learning to talk to myself with more nurturing words. Nights were the hardest, but I survived. Joe's belongings have been shared or saved. Memorials have been established. I've made new friends. My affairs are more in order. Much of the guilt has been released. I am learning to take better care of myself. I have found strength to go on. I've come a long way.

WHERE AM I NOW? I'm not the same as I was before Joe died. I now am a person in my own right, not sharing an identity role with another. Without being selfish or totally self-centered, I place more value on myself. I am beginning to experience today as being more important than yesterday or tomorrow. My proven strength is intact; I can draw on it. I value relationships more and the quality of interaction. Therefore, I choose friends more wisely. I can touch the depth of others' grief, but I cannot take it from them. I am more calm and centered. I can keep my memories and love for Joe while choosing a new life for myself.

WHERE DO I WANT TO GO AND HOW? I choose to continue the positives I've begun: good health habits, nurturing self-talk, pleasure in the moment, and quality relationships. My primary direction, however, is to add more meaning and purpose to my life. I choose to do this by returning to my field of work and selecting a specialty, continuing to write, reconnecting with my family in more mutually fulfilling ways, and deepening my religious faith and outreach.

Goals need to be stated in measurable terms. The areas described above each deserve a page where I can list specific actions to reach each goal. I also need to find ways to check my progress at specified intervals. The doing is up to me.

**Summary Statement:** Have BELIEF in myself, FAITH in God, and HOPE for the future. Then TAKE ACTION.

# NEW YEAR'S DAY

*Can Be Any Day*

I take stock:


WHERE HAVE I BEEN?



WHERE AM I NOW?



WHERE DO I WANT TO GO AND HOW?



**Summary Statement:**

# Recommended Reading and Resources

## BOOKS

CELEBRATE YOUR SELF
*Enhancing Your Self-Esteem*
Dorothy Corkille Briggs
Published in 1971, this remains a favorite book about
personal growth.

THE COURAGE TO GRIEVE
*Creative Living, Recovery & Growth through Grief*
Judy Tatelbaum
Deals with all aspects of grief and its resolution. Easy to
read and very practical.

THE COURAGE TO LAUGH
*Humor, Hope and Healing in the Face of Death and Dying*
Allen Klein
The author shows how to face the grieving process with
dignity, compassion, and yes, even laughter.

CRY UNTIL YOU LAUGH
*Comforting Guidance for Coping with Grief*
Richard J. Obershaw
Mixes humor with solid, practical advice in a down-to-
earth approach that has helped thousands of people.
As useful to clergy, funeral directors, and healthcare
professionals as to the bereaved themselves.

FINDING YOUR WAY AFTER YOUR SPOUSE DIES
Marta Felber
The author invites grieving readers to join her for informal conversations about how they might deal with their
grief. There are sixty-four short "visits." Guided prayers
and scripture references at the end of each chapter add
another dimension to the book.

GETTING THROUGH THE NIGHT
*Finding Your Way after the Loss of a Loved One*
Eugenia Price
A short book with a deep message: through God's strength,
we can one day learn to live again in the morning light.

GETTING TO THE OTHER SIDE OF GRIEF
*Overcoming the Loss of a Spouse*
Susan J. Zonnebelt-Smeenge and Robert C. De Vries
Written from two different perspectives. She is a psycholo-
gist, he a theologian; both were widowed at a relatively
young age. They share their stories to prove that grief, if
worked through properly, leads to a fresh new start.

GRIEF
*A Natural Reaction to Loss*
Marge Eaton Heegaard
This simple guide helps the bereaved understand that
their personal reaction to the death of a loved one is part
of a natural process.

GRIEVING THE LOSS OF SOMEONE YOU LOVE
*Daily Meditations to Help You through the Grieving Process*
Raymond Mitsch and Lynn Brookside
Through a series of seventy daily devotions, this book
shares wisdom, insight, and comfort that will help you
through and beyond your grief.

HOW TO SURVIVE THE LOSS OF A LOVE
Melba Colgrove, Harold H. Bloomfield, and
Peter McWilliams
A bestseller with ninety-four suggestions for surviving,
healing, and growing.

I'M GRIEVING AS FAST AS I CAN
*How Young Widows and Widowers Can Cope and Heal*
Linda Feinberg
Speaks to the unique needs and challenges of the
young widowed.

IN SICKNESS AND IN HEALTH
*One Woman's Story of Love, Loss, and Healing*
Gail Lynch
In this well-crafted memoir, a woman recounts her husband's battle with terminal brain cancer. Readers will
find emotional support and healing comfort as they join
the author on her journey through grief and recovery.

THE JOURNEY THROUGH GRIEF
*Reflections of Healing*
Alan D. Wolfelt
This spiritual companion encourages mourners to think
with the heart and the soul. It carries an affirming message
of faith, hope, and healing. It is adaptable for use in a
group setting.

LIVING WHEN A LOVED ONE HAS DIED
Earl A. Grollman
Gently, honestly, and with simple compassion, the author
says what must be said to help readers confront death
and go on living.

## MOURNING & MITZVAH
*A Guided Journal for Walking the Mourner's Path through Grief to Healing*
Anne Brener
With an emphasis on hope and growth, the mourner is led, in easy-to-follow steps, through the mourning process. Equally helpful to those outside the Jewish tradition.

## ON YOUR OWN
*A Widow's Passage to Emotional & Financial Well-Being*
Alexandra Armstrong and Mary R. Donahue
Authors profile four women at ages forty-three, fifty, sixty-two, and seventy-five to examine different life situations and needs. Very practical help is provided.

## REMEMBERING WITH LOVE
*Messages for the First Year of Grieving and Beyond.*
Elizabeth Levang and Sherokee Isle
An affirming gift for those grieving the loss of a loved one, this book offers compassion, comfort, and guidance. More than three hundred short pieces remind us that we are not alone, and that we can survive.

## SEASONS OF GRIEF AND HEALING
James E. Miller
A gift book for those who have lost a loved one. Provides inspiring passages from poetry, literature, and the Bible; compassionate exploration of feelings; and simple renewal activities.

## SWALLOWED BY A SNAKE
*The Gift of the Masculine Side of Healing*
Thomas R. Golden
An excellent guide for understanding and undertaking the masculine path of healing.

## A TIME TO GRIEVE
*Meditations for Healing after the Death of a Loved One*
Carol Staudacher
Comforting, down-to-earth thoughts and meditations—including the authentic voices of survivors—for anyone grieving the loss of a loved one. Each page is complete in itself and can be read in order or at random.

## WHEN A LIFEMATE DIES
*Stories of Love, Loss, and Healing*
Edited by Susan Heinlein, Grace Brumett, and Jane Tibbals
This moving collection of heartfelt stories, poems, essays, and journal entries recounts the real experiences of real people who have had to face the death of a lifemate.

## WHEN BAD THINGS HAPPEN TO GOOD PEOPLE
Rabbi Harold S. Kushner
This classic self-help guide explains how to find comfort and strength in the face of tragedy while understanding God's role in recovery.

## WIDOW TO WIDOW
*Thoughtful, Practical Ideas for Rebuilding Your Life*
Genevieve Ginsburg
A book that explores challenges after the death of a mate. Includes a section on the special needs of young widowed persons as well as a survival checklist.

# BOOKS FOR SPECIAL NEEDS

## A DECEMBERED GRIEF
*Living with Loss While Others Are Celebrating*
Harold Ivan Smith and Alan D. Wolfelt
With keen perception, this book provides illustrations and insights for those facing fresh grief during the holidays. Written from a Christian perspective.

## A GARDEN OF LOVE AND HEALING
*Living Tributes to Those We Have Loved and Lost*
Marsha Olson
Creative ideas for setting aside a special section of the garden to honor those who have touched our lives. Includes information on symbolic plants and flowers, planting a tree in a loved one's honor, thematic garden accents, and informal ceremonies for dedicating your memory garden.

## THE GRIEVING TEEN
*A Guide for Teenagers and Their Friends*
Helen Fitzgerald
Discusses the emotional impact of bereavement on young men and women who are simultaneously struggling through the difficult transition from childhood to adulthood. Also covers "survivor's guilt," problems in school, and changes in family relationships and friendships.

## GUIDING YOUR CHILD THROUGH GRIEF
Mary Ann Emswiler and James P. Emswiler
Based on their experiences as counselors—and as parents of grieving children—the authors help ease the uncertainty and helplessness that parents commonly feel as they reach out to their mourning children. Specific advice is given. Highly recommended.

## HELPING THE BEREAVED CHILD
*Grief Gardening, Growth through Grief, and Other Touchstones for Caregivers*
Alan D. Wolfelt
Practical guidelines and insights are offered on how a grieving child thinks, feels, and mourns; what makes each child's grief unique; how the bereaved child heals; helping grieving children at school; helping the grieving adolescent; and self-care for the child's caregiver.

## HELP ME SAY GOODBYE
*Activities for Helping Kids Cope When a Special Person Dies*
Janis Silverman
An art therapy and activity book for young children coping with the death of a loved one. Each activity helps children express themselves through different stages of grief.

## HOLIDAY HOPE
*Remembering Loved Ones During Special Times of the Year*
Compiled by the editors of Fairview Press, with illustrations by Randy Sholes
Advice, stories, poems, activities, and music to help those coping with grief during holidays and other special times of the year, including birthdays and anniversaries.

## I WASN'T READY TO SAY GOODBYE
Noel Brook & Pamela Blair
Thoughtful, thorough, and intensely meaningful. Those struggling to cope with the sudden death of a loved one will easily relate to this book.

## MEDITATION MADE EASY
*An Introduction to the Basics of the Ancient Art of Meditation*
Lorin Roche
A comprehensive book to help you learn how to meditate, overcome obstacles to your practice, and make meditation both natural and vital.

## NEW COMPLETE DO-IT-YOURSELF MANUAL
Reader's Digest
A comprehensive, up-to-date resource for do-it-yourself projects. Contains over 500 pages and more than 4,000 illustrations.

## NO TIME FOR GOODBYES
*Coping with Sorrow, Anger, and Injustice after a Tragic Death*
Janice Harris Lord
This book is devoted to the unique grief suffered when a loved one dies a sudden and violent death. It provides self-affirming skills for emotional expression that will help survivors get well again.

## WHAT COLOR IS YOUR PARACHUTE?
*A Practical Manual for Job-Hunters and Career-Changers*
Richard N. Bolles
For nearly thirty years, this book has been the guiding light for those in pursuit of satisfying and fulfilling employment.

## THE WIDOW'S RESOURCE
*How to Solve the Financial and Legal Problems That Occur within the First Six to Nine Months of Your Husband's Death*
Julie A. Calligaro
Guides the newly widowed through legal and financial problems. Contains sample letters and to-do lists on perforated pages that tear out for easy use.

# MAIL-ORDER BOOKS, MAGAZINES, AND OTHER GRIEF MATERIALS

ACCORD
1941 Bishop Lane
Suite 202
Louisville, KY 40218
(800) 346-3087
www.Accordinc.org
e-mail: Sherry@Accordinc.org

BEREAVEMENT
*A Magazine of Hope and Healing*
Bereavement Publishing, Inc.
4765 North Carefree Circle
Colorado Springs, CO 80917
(888) 604-4673
www.bereavementmag.com
e-mail: grief@bereavementmag.com

CENTERING CORPORATION
1531 North Saddle Creek Road
Omaha, NE 68104
(402) 553-1200
www.webhealing.com/centering

COMPASSION BOOKS
477 Hannah Branch Road
Burnsville, NC 28714
(800) 970-4220
www.compassionbooks.com
e-mail: heal2grow@aol.com

WILLOWGREEN
10351 Dawson's Creek Boulevard
Suite B
Fort Wayne, IN 46825
(260) 490-2222
www.willowgreen.com
jmiller@willowgreen.com

# ORGANIZATIONS

AARP GRIEF AND LOSS PROGRAMS
601 E Street NW
Washington, DC 20049
(800) 424-3410 or (202) 434-2260
(866) 797-2277 Grief Support Line
www.griefandloss.org
e-mail: griefandloss@aarp.org
Serves bereaved persons and their families through a wide variety of programs, including one-to-one outreach (such as its Widowed Persons Service), support groups, and educational meetings. Call for a free copy of "On Being Alone."

ALLIANCE FOR RETIRED AMERICANS
888 16th Street NW
Washington, DC 20006
(888) 373-6497
www.retiredamericans.org
Information on housing, nursing homes, long-term care, prescription drugs, Social Security, and patients' rights.

AMERICAN ASSOCIATION OF PASTORAL COUNSELORS
9504A Lee Highway
Fairfax, VA 22031-2303
(703) 385-6967
www.aapc.org
e-mail: info@aapc.org
A pastoral care referral service to help you find a center or counselor in your area.

THE AMERICAN PSYCHIATRIC ASSOCIATION
1400 K Street NW
Washington, DC 20005
(888) 357-7924
www.psych.org
e-mail: apa@psych.org
Ask for the number to the district branch in your state, which will give you the names of doctors in your area.

THE AMERICAN PSYCHOLOGICAL ASSOCIATION
750 First Street NE
Washington, DC 20002-4242
(800) 374-2721 or (202) 336-5500
www.apa.org
e-mail: public.affairs@apa.org
Ask for the number of the executive officer serving your state. That person will refer you to therapists in your area.

THE DOUGY CENTER
P.O. Box 86582
Portland, OR 97286
(503) 775-5683
www.grievingchild.org
e-mail: help@dougy.org
Provides telephone assistance and literature to widowed persons with children and adolescents. Maintains a national directory of children's grief services and will refer you to resources in your area.

THE ELDERCARE LOCATOR
(800) 677-1116
www.eldercare.gov
A public service of the U.S. Administration on Aging, with a Web site and toll-free number for locating more than 4,800 service providers. Areas of assistance include adult daycare and respite services, nursing home ombudsman assistance, consumer fraud, in-home care complaints, legal services, elder abuse/protective services, Medicaid/Medigap information, tax assistance, and transportation.

NATIONAL ASSOCIATION OF SOCIAL WORKERS
750 First Street NE
Suite 700, Washington, DC 20002-4241
(202) 408-8600
www.socialworkers.org
Call or visit the Web site to obtain the names of registered clinical social workers in your area.

PARENTS WITHOUT PARTNERS
Information Center
1650 South Dixie Highway
Suite 500
Boca Raton, FL 33432-7461
(800) 637-7974
www.parentswithoutpartners.org
Parents without Partners provides single parents and their children an opportunity to enhance self-confidence and sensitivity toward others. It offers a supportive environment for developing friendships and sharing parenting techniques. Call or visit the Web site to locate a chapter in your area.

SENIORNET
121 Second Street
7th Floor
San Francisco, CA 94105
415-495-4990
www.seniornet.org
SeniorNet is a nonprofit organization for adults fifty and older. Members learn and teach others to use computers and communications technologies to accomplish a variety of tasks. There are over 200 learning centers throughout the United States. Membership is not required to participate in the SeniorNet RoundTable discussion on the Web site.

WOMEN WORK!
The National Network for Women's Employment
1625 K Street NW
Suite 300
Washington, DC 20006
(800) 235-2732 or (202) 467-6346
www.womenwork.org
e-mail: womenwork@womenwork.org
Women Work! Programs are nationally known for their effectiveness in helping women find and keep jobs to support their families. This organization will help locate job-training programs that make women employable and will sometimes offer job referrals.

YWCA
The YWCA provides services to women entering or reentering the job market. Services include employability and employment training, temporary housing, counseling, educational classes, and general support. Check your local directory for specific programs at your nearest YWCA.

# Index

Printed in the United States
123409LV00001B/39/A